They Lie, We Lie

Getting on with anthropology

Peter Metcalf

London and New York

First published 2002
by Routledge
11 New Fetter Lane, London EC4P 4EE

Simultaneously published in the USA and Canada
by Routledge
29 West 35th Street, New York NY 10001

Routledge is an imprint of the Taylor & Francis Group

Peter Metcalf has conducted research in Borneo for over
two decades. He is Professor of Anthropology at the
University of Virginia, USA.

Typeset in Sabon by BC Typesetting, Bristol
Printed and bound in Great Britain by
TJ International, Padstow, Cornwall

British Library Cataloguing in Publication Data
A catalogue record for this book is available from the British Library

Library of Congress Cataloging in Publication Data
A catalog record for this book has been requested

ISBN 0–415–26259–3 (hbk)
ISBN 0–415–26260–7 (pbk)

Malut dé, malut kita
They lie, we lie

How am I to read this gesture?

She was for years an obstacle; a tiny woman with great authority, old even when I first knew her in the mid-1970s, who did not want me to know certain things, who wanted certain knowledge to die with her. She puzzled me then, although I think I understand her better now. Nevertheless, I had to circumvent her, and that is what I did, using every dodge I could find. Now I hear that she is very frail and cannot last much longer, and also something more surprising: I hear that she has left instructions that a copy of my book, carefully wrapped in plastic, be put in her coffin. How am I to read this gesture? Is she finally embracing my project of documentation? Or is she burying it? Is she taking her secret world with her after all, despite my best efforts?

Contents

Illustrations

1 Lies

This is an essay about lies: white lies and ones black as night, evasions, exaggerations, delusions, half-truths, and credible denials. Consequently, it is about art and literature, and specifically the art and literature of anthropology, as ambiguously manifested in our unique genre, the ethnography. It is a response from one discipline to the pervasive epistemological skepticism of our times. At the beginning of the twenty-first century, it is swimming against the intellectual tide to discuss the truths that ethnographies may contain, so let us instead see what profit there is in examining the kinds of lies in which they traffic.

It is a matter not only of lies told *by* anthropologists, however, but also of lies told *to* anthropologists. There is nothing self-evident about why anyone would bother talking to the would-be ethnographer – assuming they do – except perhaps for polite platitudes. In unfamiliar surroundings, he or she is usually socially inept, and often linguistically incompetent. Such people are generally avoided. Yet ethnographies are full of obliging informants, hastening to play Sancho Panza to the ethnographer's Don Quixote. We have to ask ourselves what transactions of power and knowledge underlie their motives.

Moreover, having admitted informants, the presumed culture bearers, into the equations of deceit, we have to consider the conceptual premises and conversational constraints under which they select what to tell and how to tell it. Here again, nothing is self-evident.

"Something spoken which is not true"

Eve Danziger (1997) recounts a salutary experience among the Mopan Maya of Belize. To entertain some friends, she showed on VCR a cartoon version of Rudyard Kipling's *The Jungle Book*.[1] This was well received because it was interpretable even to the old people watching, but there were things that bothered them. At the beginning of the movie, the infant Mowgli is abandoned in the forest and raised by wild beasts. Later, he is seen playing happily with panthers and bears. Why, asked Danziger's friends, didn't the animals eat the child? Finally someone asked doubtfully if all this were really "true" – *jaj* in Mopan Maya. When told that it was not, her friends were shocked, even offended, and showed no further interest in the movie.

At first blush, this reaction seems only naive, and perhaps charmingly so – a more extreme version of the confusion that fans often display between a film star and the character he or she plays. (Groucho Marx claimed that the question he was most often asked was whether Harpo really could talk.) Danziger insists, however, that the reaction she encountered ran far deeper than this. In the first place, there are Mopan stories (*kwenta*) that do not seem so very different to *The Jungle Book*, concerning such things as half-human creatures who live in the forest, or the marriage of the sun and moon, but these stories are believed to be "strictly true." Made-up stories are dismissed as *baxul*, "games" or "toys," suitable only for children. Stories that are discovered to be untrue – fictions – are simply *tus*, "something spoken which is not true" (Danziger 1997: 4–9).

Knowing this much about *kwenta*, the reflex of someone with my training in the century-old anthropological tradition of theorizing about religion is to conclude that they are "sacred" texts. But this does not in fact get us very far. The stories are not particularly hedged about with taboos, nor situated in the midst of ritual, nor do they seem to tell any fundamental "truths." Instead they are told for entertainment. There are no supernatural sanctions on errors, but skill at recounting them is appreciated. Viewed from this angle, the stories begin to resemble our notion of literature rather than esoteric lore, but there remains that awkward insistence that they recount literal truth.

This combination of truth and art is evidently difficult for Westerners, so much so that at the end of the nineteenth century Oscar Wilde could make a running joke of it. In *The Importance of Being Earnest*, Lady Bracknell responds to an accusation: "Untruthful! My nephew Algernon? Impossible! He is an Oxonian." What provokes the accusation is a fictional brother, made up to provide excuses for not attending tedious social events, but the author of the fiction is unabashed: "To invent anything at all is an act of sheer genius, and, in a commercial age like ours show considerable physical courage. Few of our modern novelists care to invent a single thing." In "The Decay of Lying" his protagonist inveighs against the modern novelist, who "presents us with dull facts under the guise of fiction." Warming to his theme, he urges:

> People have a careless way of talking about a "born liar," just as they talk about a born poet. But in both cases they are wrong. Lying and poetry are arts – arts, as Plato saw, not unconnected with each other – and they require the most careful study, the most disinterested devotion.
>
> (Wilde 1994 [1891]: 375, 972)

The *fin-de-siècle* skepticism of the next century might seem to have left little room for Wilde's teasing, but it was noticeable that any talk of the artistry of ethnography still made us shift uncomfortably in our chairs, because it implied an equivocation with truth. An anthropology in Mopan would presumably not be encumbered with this implication.

Danziger, however, sees a different significance in Mopan attitudes to fiction, reflecting her background in linguistics. She finds a whole concept of speaking that is radically different to our own, one that challenges common assumptions about the nature of "speech act." In contrast to most linguistic theory, Mopan do not place emphasis on individual agency and the speaker's creativity. Instead, they explicitly stress the role of the hearers, and their obligation is to believe. Speakers must respect that intention in their hearers. "Something spoken which is not true" constitutes a rent in the social fabric; it is antisocial, and judged as such.

Mopan are not unique in their credulity. A body of research in social psychology has tested the reactions of experimental subjects to implausible or inconsistent claims, and confirmed a pervasive tendency of hearers to believe what they are told (DePaulo *et al.* 1996; Kashy and DePaulo 1996). This applies even to boasting (Schenkler and Leary 1982). Moreover, even when subjects had grounds to doubt statements, they tended to reduce the effect of claims rather than discounting them entirely (Jones 1979). This no doubt explains the curious tendency in academia for those who make the most inflated claims of originality and importance for their work – I name no names – to be most rewarded by the attention of their peers.

What differentiates Mopan reactions is the clear assignment of blame exclusively to the liar. They could never be induced to chuckle conspiratorially at P.T. Barnum's famous maxim: "a sucker born every minute." For them, trust is a higher social value than sophistication. Instead, they have a battery of conversational techniques – introductory caveats and explanatory preambles – designed to avoid the disrespect of misleading people, even unintentionally (Danziger 1997: 15–16). One can only wonder at such scrupulous honesty, and hope that it confers a special resistance to the hype of advertising to which the rest of us are so weakly vulnerable.

At the same time, however, it is hard to imagine how everyday conversation proceeds in the face of such demanding literalism. What room can there be for humor, or irony, or any form of verbal play? Thinking about the conventions that surround a staged drama, Danziger remarks:

By saying that Mopan reject the sort of experience common in the Euro-American theatre then, I am saying that this is a society in which (these levels of) metaphor and analogy are explicitly rejected as legitimate branches of self-conscious poetic expression.

(1997: 11)

Justifiably, she sees her findings as subversive of current theories of cognition that take metaphor as a fundamental and universal vehicle of thought (Lakoff and Johnson 1980). They seem equally challenging to those theories of ritual and social action influential in the 1970s that relied on a dramaturgical analogy (Goffman 1963; Turner 1974). Meanwhile, care and modesty characterize Mopan sociality, and Danziger notes the "acceptability of silence in Mopan conversation" (1997: 16).

They lie, we lie

Nothing could be further from truth in the longhouses of central northern Borneo, among the Upriver People (*Orang Ulu*), where conversation flows as freely as the tumbling rivers. Longhouses seem designed to promote it: hundreds of people living under one roof, and no possibility of privacy, even if such a thing were conceived of, let alone desired. A wide veranda stretching the length of the house on the side facing the river is communal space, and people pass along it constantly, or gather to work together or socialize. On the landward side there is a row of family apartments, each opening on to the veranda, but even they are crowded with residents, and open to a constant flow of visitors.

When I began fieldwork there, in a Berawan longhouse at Long Teru, I soon learned that my hosts would not tolerate interviews using an interpreter. They valued conversation too much for that, and they would go to sleep, or wander off, rather than wait for the next round of translation. But in impromptu exchanges while bathing in the river, or strolling along the veranda, they would engage in rapid-fire joking and repartee. I never felt like anything other than a dullard in their company. They can tease mercilessly, enough to provoke tears of anger in grown men. (Women are seldom victimized to this extent.) Nor is satire restricted to verbal behavior: a favorite form of entertainment is to recall some gaffe or piece of clumsiness made by someone in the audience, and to jump up and act it out, complete with exaggerated gestures and foolish expressions. The imitator is immediately followed by another, and another, each adding new absurdities, concluding, in the most gratifying cases, with the victim himself.[2] Even at rituals held inside family apartments or out on the veranda hilarity would often disrupt the rites themselves, and always they had to compete with the general hubbub of the crowd. In fact, a ritual was judged a failure that did not generate a noisy and uninhibited conviviality.

Not all vocalization is frivolous, however. At the other end of the spectrum are the formidable chants, sacred in the fullest Durkheimian sense, that are heard only during death rituals. Incorrectly or improperly performed, even in tiny snatches, they have the power to kill. Not surprisingly, the bulk of Berawan interactions lie somewhere between these poles of levity and weightiness. Though I made no special study of them, there are characteristic Berawan modes of gossip and debate and so on. For obvious reasons, however, I paid closest attention to the genres of narration. Some of the stories my enquiries provoked were short, some long, most were informal and subject to constant interruptions by anyone who came by to hear what was going on. But sometimes I was met with the insistence that I consult a particular expert, and arrange a full and proper telling.

My contribution to these gatherings was usually a bottle or two of *arak*, a potent distilled liquor sometimes made in the longhouse, but nowadays often bought in a trade store. The prestation of *arak* indicated simultaneously the formality of these occasions and their essential sociality. The audience comprised adults from neighboring rooms, and children from up and down the longhouse, little gangs of boys or girls of about the same age, who routinely passed the night in whatever room they happened to be when sleep overcame them. The hosts provided glasses and snacks and perhaps more *arak*, and only after some time did the storyteller introduce the evening's agenda. Then the crowd would draw around, their faces lit by a wick lantern, and I would get out my notebook. The children began with rapt attention, and slowly dropped off, one by one, while the adults settled down to hear the story out, chewing betel, participating as required, and occasionally turning to explain something to me. From those slow and gentle evenings I gained a great deal of information, even if I did not follow everything. They were not, however, held for my benefit; they had occurred before I arrived at Long Teru, and they had an established literary form and social function.

There was a moment in those evenings when the narrator signalled his or her readiness to begin. I remember best one particular exponent, an old woman named Bilo (i.e. "Widow") Kasi, who always began in the same way: she would fuss for a while getting comfortable, and asking people whether they had what they needed, then she would clear her throat, and, when she had everyone's attention, announce in a firm voice the formula that provides my title:

Malut dé, malut kita.

The verb *malut* means "to lie," *dé* is the third-person plural pronoun, and *kita* is the first-person plural pronoun; hence "they lie, we lie." We should note also that Berawan, in common with many Austronesian languages, has verbs that do not inflect for tense. Consequently, it could as easily be "have lied" or "will lie" as "am lying." So much for literal translation.

The phrase is surprising because it seems an odd moment to be talking about lying, but it cannot be shrugged off. On the contrary, it was clearly designed to accomplish exactly what Mikhail Bakhtin describes as the function of such openers, namely to establish the "stylistic aura" of the entire speech genre (Bakhtin 1986: 87–9).

If we take Kasi to be saying "they lied before, now I'm lying," or something amounting to "it's all lies anyway," then the aura she establishes is one of profound skepticism towards all traditional knowledge.

This is the more inescapable in that Kasi cannot mean to imply that these stories are only what we might call fairy tales, some variant of "once upon a time." Certainly her audience was partly made up of children – to begin with at least – but they were explicitly there to be instructed, not lulled to sleep.[3] Moreover, the didactic quality was only slightly less obvious for the adults. It took no great familiarity with the Berawan world view to be confident that "they" are the ancestors, if only because the stories all concerned the doings of the ancestors: who migrated from here to there, and what adventures occurred along the way; in short, the familiar anthropological category of "oral history." In the most chronologically remote episodes there were heroes who carved out river valleys and climbed to the stars, but as they grew closer to the present they took on a comfortingly factual quality – exactly the material I needed to unravel the tangled ethnological relations between the different communities. Meanwhile, those same ancestors stand at the very core of Berawan religion. They were invariably invoked in prayer, more so than the deities (Metcalf 1989: 64–8), and it was their awful presence at death rituals that made the death songs so dangerously sacred. The parallel structure of the phrase, with its repeated verb, is in itself suggestive of ritual language. No, Kasi was not telling fairy stories.

There is, however, another equally significant connotation to her phrase. In opposition to "they" stands a "we" that includes the speaker. Clearly, it means that small cohort of older people who know enough to relate Berawan tradition authoritatively. They stand between the ancestors and the audience. Perhaps what Kasi means to say is "if they lied, then I lie too." In other words, she will tell the stories just as she heard them herself, sitting as her audience now does, before storytellers long since dead. In this way, Kasi makes herself the mouthpiece of the ancestors, and assumes something of their power.

Getting on with anthropology

What strikes me as quintessentially Berawan about Kasi's phrase is its perfect balance between, on the one hand, a refusal to be impressed by anyone's revealed truths, even their own, and, on the other, a pride in the community's traditions bordering on chauvinism. The phrase produces mentally the same effect as a figure–ground reversal produces optically. Skepticism – empowerment; they replace each other instantaneously.

The attitudes to truth that the phrase succinctly expresses stand in stark contrast to those that Danziger found among the Mopan Maya. With its insistence on speaking as close as it possibly can to the literal truth at all times, Mopan discourse constitutes, on the level of what Claude Lévi-Strauss (1968) called *pensée sauvage*, an analogue of scientific discourse. The Mopan are thorough-going positivists. Meanwhile, the Berawan are just as thoroughly postmodern. Their notion of truth is dialogic in the fullest Bakhtinian sense; it exists only as a succession of mutually constructing speech events. Kasi's formula might serve as a dedication to Jacques Lyotard's influential essay *The Postmodern Condition: A Report on Knowledge* (1984), often taken as the manifesto of postmodernist philosophy, which proposes a model of knowledge as a kind of word game.

Kasi's skepticism fits neatly with the iconoclast mood of postmodernism, but there is that other connotation of her phrase, one that runs directly counter to postmodernism's nihilist tendencies. Evidently, for many postmodernists, their broad attack on the dichotomy of subject and object, the knower and the known, designed to topple Western science and Humanism, rushes on inevitably to a position in which, in Robert Scholes' words, "since there is no truth, there is no error either, and all beliefs are equal"

(1989: 56). Some embrace this position (Vattimo 1988), while others temporize (Levin and Kroker 1984), but the paralyzing effects of nihilism remain. Whatever impact this has on physicists studying nuclear particles or cosmologists theorizing about the Big Bang, the effect is devastating in anthropology, where there have always been anxieties about how far the observer can or should be removed from the observed.

Meanwhile, there is here a familiar logical conundrum of the type: all generalizations are *ipso facto* false. Those who assert unknowability assume a position of knowing. Even if they try then to relativize their own position, claiming that their position is only one of many, they must still assert that *that* is true. As Pauline Rosenau concludes: "There is simply no logical escape from this contradiction except to remain silent" (1992: 90). This formal argument resonates eerily with ethnographic strategies: anthropology has a long tradition of relativism, that is, the insistence that other world views be taken seriously, in their own terms, and not dismissed as error. True, there have been schools of anthropology that have not been relativist, and there are limitations on relativism, but the strategy remains. When, however, postmodernists are said to "relativize" their claims to knowing, they suggest an especial anthropological version of nihilism, the assertion that it is fundamentally impossible to know anything or say anything about another culture. This can lead to a kind of introverted essentialism, which authorizes ethnographers only to work in "their own culture," however that may be constructed. In this way, anthropology's traditional strategy of taking people outside themselves is inverted. Alternatively, it can produce a kind of esoteric apathy, based on the proposition that those who know do not speak, and those who speak do not know.

Postmodernist critiques were intended to prevent "business as usual" in Western scholarship, including anthropology. Not surprisingly then, they have a distracting effect on those who – for one reason or another – want somehow to get on with anthropology. For graduate students keen both to keep abreast of current theoretical developments and to begin their own projects, it can amount to a personal crisis. It makes more difficult what was always perilous: the abrupt transition from a cosy classroom world, surrounded by teachers and fellow students, to the lonely self-doubts of the novice fieldworker. The risks are not proportional to the geographical distance from home, and just as many students fail in urban situations as in jungles and deserts. Even most established professionals will confess, at least in private, that there were moments when they wondered if they would make it through their fieldwork.

For those of us who did somehow negotiate the transition, there is seldom much sense of triumph. Instead there are regrets about lost opportunities and unfulfilled relationships. Fieldwork is a profoundly humbling experience, and its effects persist. Poring over our fieldnotes, there is plenty of time to discover crucial questions that we failed to ask, and remember kindnesses that can never be repaid. These are the preliminaries to writing ethnography. Then comes the business of sorting a tangled mass of inchoate data into some kind of presentable form. All this is daunting, and a surprising number of fieldworkers fail ever to publish an ethnography. Those of us who are getting on with anthropology have faced this trial repeatedly, and the contemporary critique of ethnography has made it hard to find a way even to begin. For many nowadays it feels like trying to pick up a heavy object while simultaneously fending off a snappy dog.

There are people, however, who have no professional interest in the discipline, and who nevertheless want to get on with anthropology enough to hear what it has to tell, without being sucked into a vortex of epistemological anxieties. Contemporary anthropology has signally failed to reach these people effectively. We may remind ourselves ruefully that anthropology's all-time best seller is James Frazer's *The Golden Bough*, originally published in 1890, a book that is not so much politically incorrect as quaintly archaic. Who is there now to replace Margaret Mead as a public figure, unless it is perhaps Derek Freeman? The result is that we leave the job of popularizing anthropology to hacks, and grind our teeth at crass sensationalism. Let me pick a few examples from those that have most irritated me.

Surely there is nowhere in the world more rigidly stereotyped than Borneo. Even the tabloid press makes use of it. I once saw a front-page story in the *National Enquirer*, complete with faked photograph, reporting that Martians had landed on earth. Naive aliens that they were, however, they made the mistake of touching down in Borneo, so only their shrunken heads remained to be discovered by scientists.[4] Much of the vast travel literature on Borneo is little better. I offer in evidence *Panjamon: I Was a Headhunter* (Domalain 1974), described on the back cover as follows:

> Jean-Yves Domalain, a young scientist who loves adventure, never anticipated an adventure like this! Captured by Borneo headhunters. Forced to suffer the agonies of tribal initiation. Compelled to marry the chief's daughter. Then hunting, fishing and loving with his headhunter relatives. And finally, his life threatened by the tribe's witchdoctor, making a miraculous escape.

This is not so much lies as libelous.

Not all travel literature on Borneo is this bad, but it does return insistently to the same theme. A few examples: Bock, *Headhunters of Borneo* (1881); Furness, *Homelife of Borneo Headhunters* (1902); Cator, *Everyday Life among the Headhunters* (1905); Combinaire, *Au pays des coupeurs des têtes* (1910); Krohn, *In Borneo Jungles: Among Dayak Headhunters* (1927); Mjoberg, *Borneo: L'Île des chasseurs des têtes* (1934); Ivanhoff, *Chez les coupeurs des têtes* (1955); Wynn-Sargent, *My Life among Headhunters* (1974). The list is far from complete; a century of relentless repetition! Despite the ecological disasters that have overtaken the island in the last two decades and the social disruption they have brought about, travel books in the heroic explorer mode continue to be cranked out. For some years, I reviewed them regularly for the *Times Literary Supplement*. Some were responsible, others less so, but at no time was anything other than travelogue given to me to review, nothing about the politics or history of the island, let alone its ethnology. Evidently Borneo is a place reserved for "exploration." Another example of casual stereotyping in self-consciously intellectual publications comes from the fashionable literary magazine *Granta*, in a piece of reportage by Richard Parry (1998) about ethnic violence between Madurese people resettled by the Indonesian government in Western Kalimantan and the local population. The violence is real enough, but the emphasis of the article is entirely on the headhunting propensities of Bornean people, and has nothing to say about the political abuses that brought about the ethnic strife in the first place. My view of it is that the people of interior Borneo are the victims of violence and repression rather than the perpetrators of it, and the stereotypes of them still bandied about everywhere, in places both highbrow and lowbrow, ought to be as outdated as the image of the scalp-hunting Red Indian.

For me to make this complaint, however, is classically to take on the role of representing Bornean peoples, in addition to re-presenting them. The tendency for the two activities to become amalgamated has often been taken as evidence of the objectification by anthropologists of "their" people (for example in Spivak 1994: 70). I might well be asked who in Borneo appointed me spokesman, or authorized my version of things. Among those at war with Western Cartesian subjectivity, disillusionment is so complete that they would anyway see little difference between my rendition of Borneo and the *National Enquirer*'s. Whether or not this is seen as a *reductio ad absurdum* provides a nice test of anthropology's standing nowadays. As a *coup de grâce*, they might also point out that I too have written about headhunting (Metcalf 1996), which makes me no less implicated in sensationalism.

There is no doubting the force of such an attack, to which many anthropologists are vulnerable. Let me answer personally, however. First, I claim boldly that I was in fact, in some small degree, authorized to represent. For the two years that I lived at Long Teru, there was constant discussion on what I was really doing there. I strove to distinguish myself from the missionaries who were the only other foreigners who stayed upriver for any length of time. Consequently, popular opinion concluded – unknown to me – that I was a communist agent come to convince them to join an insurgency that rumbled on in Sarawak for two decades. This hypothesis was only disproved when my name was mentioned on the government-run radio station. Eventually, people accepted, more or less, my account of my goals, and assigned me a role accordingly: I was instructed repeatedly to "make the Berawan name big," a sort of global public relations man. It is not unusual, I would argue, for ethnographers to be asked to represent, in exactly Spivak's terms, and not only by small ethnic groups in remote places. Disempowered people everywhere will grasp at straws to gain some voice in public discourse. This indeed provides another source of guilt and regret for fieldworkers as we contemplate our failures to accomplish anything useful for people who approached us in this way.

Second, and more importantly, I deflect the attack by renouncing claims to positive knowledge or the authority of science. By the end of the twentieth century, few ethnographers in fact set out to the field with the notion that they would come home with the definitive and final answers to anything, and fewer still left that way. It is not so much that we cannot discover "facts," as that the questions that most interest us involve subtle cultural interpretations. I claim no qualitative difference between what I observe and what, say, a journalist might observe. There is a quantitative difference to be sure – no journalist could possibly take as long as we do investigating a story – but the real difference lies in what we do with our observations. For the moment, however, the point is that there is no absolute discontinuity between ethnography and other forms of reportage. Perversely, those who argue that an ethnographer has less right to point out injustices than a journalist promote the very proposition they attack: that ethnography is radically different to other forms of writing.

The same disclaimer applies to charges of sensationalism. It is undeniable that anthropology makes of the exotic, just as the tabloid press does, to attract the attention of an audience. But there is nothing in that to make us flinch. Ever since *The Golden Bough* our material has been sensational, indeed irresistible. How many dinner-table conversations, earnest or witty, wrongheaded or insightful, has it sparked over the years? How many intellectuals have been influenced by it, from psychologists like Carl Jung to poets like T.S. Eliot? Who could possibly say the same about the *National Enquirer*? However much we might now disdain Frazer's evolutionary theories, it is impossible to deny the intellectual impact of the book. Its enduring relevance comes about because Frazer not only points to strange things, but also puts them in a framework in which they signify something; that is, he engages in interpretation.

Characteristically, anthropology plays a double game with the exotic, first invoking it, and then negating it. In the first process, we build a sense of problem by showing how very different things can be in another culture. In all the social complexities of the contemporary world, it is not at all necessary that this other culture be far removed in time or space. In the second move, we set about putting the puzzling thing that we have identified into some context, that is, situating it within whatever cultural premises, social conditions, and historical circumstances we deem relevant. In so far as this produces a sense of understanding, the exotic is lost. There is then room for a third, reflexive, move, in which what was once familiar in one's own culture is in turn made to seem strange, or "defamiliarized" (Marcus and Fischer 1986: 157).

As for headhunting, it is no lie to say that the severed heads of enemies, or long-dry relics of the same, were at one time used in ritual contexts in some parts of Borneo, and even that people were murdered to furnish such trophies. Moreover, these practices are deeply mysterious, and it is a long-standing conundrum to decide what religious or historical context offers the best promise of insight. There is plenty of scope here for ethnographic analysis. There is also no difficulty in making the reflexive move, because nowadays the most common manifestation of the headhunting complex consists of panics that sweep around the interior caused by rumours that Europeans are coming to take the heads of local people. Now we might ask what it is about Western culture that strikes Bornean people as so terrifyingly predatory.

The point of this defense of representation is not, however, to brush aside criticism. On the contrary, my goal is to deal directly with some at least of the provocative issues that have caused ferment in anthropology in the last decade. As the postmodernists intended, there will indeed never be any return to the "business as usual" that operated during the 1950s and 1960s when the discipline became established, institutionally and intellectually, in its modern form. Consequently, it is necessary to confront the malaise that afflicts anthropology at this time – and particularly anthropology, because in no other discipline are epistemological dilemmas more sharp. What I want to show is the extraordinary mix in fieldwork of seeing plainly and being all at sea; that the result is more demanding than any mere text could be; and that the juxtaposition of piles of information and gulfs of incomprehension remains as compelling as ever. I want to emphasize what Kasi understood plainly, and what her phrase so neatly conveys: that all our doubts announce not the end of a story, but the beginning of one. Not being capable of a Mopan level of truth, the requirement for which would indeed silence me, I shall follow Kasi's lead, invoke skeptically my flawed ancestors, and begin.

They lie, we lie.

2 Struggle

Immediately, however, a little deception: I do not really repeat the voices of my ancestors in the way that Bilo Kasi did. I suppose I might, but it is in practice my intellectual ancestors that I invoke. Nor is it my stance that I simply repeat what they said, though I mean to preserve a close relationship with them and what they said. Even that is not the end of it, however. I also plan to repeat at least some of what Kasi told me, just as her grandchildren might do in years to come, or may in fact be doing even as I write. I graft myself on, as it were, to her ancestral root; I make her my ancestor.

Learning experiences

It is perhaps only a mild overstatement, a harmless rhetorical conceit. Nevertheless, it replicates in miniature what James Clifford describes in a famous article as a pervasive and characteristic "ethnographic allegory":

> Ethnographies often present themselves as fictions of learning, the acquisition of knowledge, and finally of authority to understand and represent another culture. The researcher begins in a child's relation to adult culture, and ends by speaking with the wisdom of experience. It is interesting to observe how, in the

text, the author's enunciative modes may shift back and forth between learning from and speaking for the other. This fictional freedom is crucial to ethnography's allegorical appeal: the simultaneous reconstruction of a culture and a knowing self, a double "coming of age in Samoa."

> (Clifford 1986: 108n,
> the quotation marks a reference to Mead 1923)

Mea culpa; this is indeed the kind of story I have to tell. It does not follow, however, that I will reproduce the same kinds of "fictions" that have been told before because learning experiences vary enormously in their effect, as every student knows, not to mention those who graduate from the proverbial "school of hard knocks." Consequently, there is something to be gained by comparing the learning experiences reported by ethnographers.

Perhaps the most famous educative relationship in all of anthropology was that between Victor Turner and his Ndembu informant Muchona. Turner repeatedly refers to Muchona as his "colleague," and speaks of the sessions that he had with him as "seminars." In accordance with that spirit of egalitarianism, he even attributes to Muchona motives similar to his own:

> A new and exhilarating intellectual dimension had opened up to him as well as to myself in our discussions of symbolism. At such times he had the bright eye of some raptor, hawk or kite as he poised over a definitive explanation. Watching him, I sometimes used to fancy that he would have been truly at home scoring debating points on a don's dais, gowned or perhaps in a habit. He delighted in making explicit what he had known subliminally about his own religion. A curious quirk of fate had brought him an audience and fellow enthusiasts of a kind he could never have encountered in the villages. In this situation, he was respected for his knowledge in his own right. What has become of him since? Can he ever be again

the man he was before he experienced the quenchless thirst for objective knowledge?

(Turner 1967: 138)

Turner's affectionate portrait of "Muchona the Hornet: Interpreter of Religion" first appeared in a collection edited by John Casagrande (1960: 131–51), but only became widely known because it was included in Turner's best-known book, *The Forest of Symbols* (1967), which, as it happens, also contains Turner's most concise statement of his method of symbolic analysis, in the essay "Symbols in Ndembu Religion." It is noticeable that Turner projects onto Muchona not only the abstract curiosity of the scholar, but also the very same mode of interpretation. It is an important premise of symbolic analysis that meanings may be revealed beyond what is explicit, as in Turner's famous inventory of the various nuances, positive and negative, often contradictory, of the multivocalic *mudyi* tree (1967: 20–5). Moreover, deep cultural significance is often attached to these discovered meanings. In this passage we have Muchona excitedly dredging up what he had previously known only "subliminally." Is it credible that Muchona really thought in this way? As for Muchona's "bright eye" as he pounced on some intepretation, whether or not it was characteristic of Muchona I cannot say, having never met the man, but I can report that it was exactly the way Turner himself looked on occasion.

The equating, not to say fusing, of the informant with the ethnographer is surely what made the figure of Muchona so widely appealing. What would most ethnographers not give for such a productive, mutually satisfactory relationship? Philippe Déscola insists that they are in practice rare: "True, some native exegetes have been known to produce systematic syntheses, but they are so few that most anthropology students know their names" (1992: 107). I read it differently, however: Muchona exists as a model and an ideal for many ethnographers. The kinds of "systematic syntheses" of which Muchona was capable – in effect, indigenous theologies – may be unusual, but reliance on native exegesis is not. Most ethnographers are at some level constantly on the look-out for at least partial reincarnations of Muchona, and in my experience a great number claim to have found them.

To underline that point, the very word "exegesis" has taken on a particular meaning in anthropology. In his methodological essay, Turner specifies three sources of data on "ritual symbols." The first comprises the rituals themselves, as observed by the ethnographer. The last is comparative contexts "worked out by the anthropologist." These are often assumed to be comparisons with other cultures, but Turner makes it clear that internal comparisons are even more important. That is to say, an interpretation suggested by one rite gains conviction if it seems to shed light on some other ritual, or a myth, from the same culture. The second source, mediating between the behavioral and the interpretive, is accounts offered by the participants themselves, whether "specialists or laymen" (Turner 1967: 20). Since Turner, "exegesis" has come to mean just this. It is synonymous with indigenous interpretation, and every use of the word conjures the figure of Muchona.

Was Kasi, then, a "native exegete"? Certainly, I learned a great deal from her, as I described in the previous chapter. But I would never have been inclined to call her a "colleague," or my visits with her "seminars." If Turner's learning experience with Muchona resembled university, mine felt more like primary school, with Kasi the severe schoolmarm. Moreover, Kasi had definite ideas about what I should and should not know. If she was my Muchona, she was a very partial one, or perhaps even the inverse of one. Thereby hangs a tale, and it is one I propose to tell in full because I can only draw out the significance of our relationship by attention to its unfolding details. My goal is to disentangle those aspects of our relationship that have to do with our eccentricities, hers and mine, from those that are inherent in the practice of anthropology. In personal terms, this allows me to confront the vague sense of having failed in fieldwork that I share with many other ethnographers.

In professional terms, it addresses those fictions, allegories, or hyperboles that Clifford talks about, and on which ethnography depends.

In working through my relationship with Kasi, the comparison with Muchona provides a useful cross-check, and here I have had the advantage of conversations with Edith Turner, whose vivid recollections of fieldwork among the Ndembu have allowed me to explore details not covered in her or her husband's writings. In addition, Victor's fieldnotes have been collected and catalogued since his death in 1984 by Sandra Bamford, under the auspices of the Shannon Center for Advanced Study at the University of Virginia. Tape-recorded interviews with Edie by Matt Engelke and myself have been added to the archive, along with her fieldnotes.

Edie's recollections of Muchona are of his high-pitched, rapid voice. Vic often found him difficult to follow, so he recruited a local schoolteacher, Windson Kashinakaji, to help him with translation and elucidation. Windson was no mere employee, however; he was keen to learn more about his own people, and consequently the three of them sitting round a table inside one of the Turners' tents did indeed have the incongruous air of a scholarly seminar, an effect that Edie smiles to remember. But where did Muchona acquire his didactic style? He was certainly a ritual specialist in a mode familiar to Ndembu themselves. His expertise was widely acknowledged, and he was often invited to assist at large rituals, where he would not hesitate to hold forth on what should happen and why. His nickname, "the Hornet" (*Iyanvu*), might suggest to us an irritating buzzing around, but Edie insists that the connotations for Ndembu were of making a point as rapidly as a hornet stinging – in short, of incisiveness.

As students of indigenous religions soon learn, however, expertise in ritual procedure does not invariably, or even frequently, extend to "exegesis." Yet it is clear from Turner's frequent verbatim quotations from him that Muchona was accustomed to taking that extra step. Edie offers a clue about why this was the case: it turns out that Victor was not the first Englishman to employ Muchona's services. In the 1910s there was a magistrate named Frank Melland stationed in the Kasempa District of what was then Northern Rhodesia (now Zambia), a District that included the Ndembu. Like many another colonial officer, he made a hobby of collecting details about local customs as he traveled about attending court sessions. It was of course for people such as him that the Royal Anthropological Society prepared its famous *Notes and Queries* as a checklist for amateur ethnographers. The book that resulted from Melland's fossicking has a sensational title, *In Witch-Bound Africa* (1923), but turns out to be a sober-sided account divided into such familiar boxes as "Childhood," "Marriage and Divorce," "Hunting," "Religion," and so on. It is the sort of book that later ethnographers seize on because it provides valuable nuggets of comparative information from an earlier date. Melland is modest in his claims to what he knows, and he acknowledges a long list of Africans who helped him, mostly local chiefs and court "messengers." Muchona does not rate a mention, however, perhaps because he was too young. Melland left the District in 1922, and it was thirty years later that Muchona met Victor Turner. By then, he was probably in his fifties (see Figure 1). Muchona himself never explained how Melland's questioning had shaped his encounter with his own religion in the years when he was making himself into a ritual expert, or how that set him on his way to becoming Victor Turner's "colleague."

It is amusing to wonder what Kasi might have made of Muchona. Judging by the way she treated me, she would not have been impressed by the supposed egalitarianism of his professional relationship with Turner. For a Western academic, especially in the colonial period, it might seem virtuous, but I suspect that Kasi would have seen it as merely presumptuous. She might well ask whether, in the allegory of ethnographic learning, the student is the equal of the teacher, and what became of the "child's relation to adult culture" (see Figure 2). To underline that, let me begin with a vignette: Kasi in disciplinary mode.

Figure 1 Muchona, top right in topi, officiating at a rite of *wubwang'u*, the twin ceremony. The "doctors" begin by each eating a small piece of cassava. Photograph previously unpublished, courtesy of the Turner Archive.

Kasi's preemptive strike

At about six months into fieldwork, I still felt unsure of myself in the community. To begin with, my linguistic abilities remained shaky, so that I was always nervous that I would make a fool of myself. In these circumstances the education of the ethnographer becomes a daily reality, and no mere allegory. It required great concentration to hang on to the thread of a conversation and that was tiring, but there was nowhere in the crowded longhouse where I could hide myself away from interaction. If I tried to read, children would pull the book down to see what I was looking at. If I pretended to sleep late, people would ask, in all kindness, if I was ill. I knew

Figure 2 Bilo Kasi with Michael Melai Usang (see page 59) at Long Teru in 1974. Photograph by author.

very well that it was perverse in me to resent such a wealth of sociability. Ethnographers elsewhere found themselves among people who lived in isolated households, or else kept outsiders rigorously at arm's length, and they were surely worse off. Even so, I doubt that anyone raised with Western middle-class attitudes to personal space can live in a longhouse without psychic discomfort.

During that time, I was gradually feeling my way around, trying to work out who was who. This was impeded by a complex etiquette having to do with names. Everyone had multiple names, teknonyms and nicknames, which were liable to be changed from time to time. As for a person's true or "body" name (*ngaran usa*), it was impolite to enquire about it. In the case of old people whose teknonyms hid their body names, I sometimes learned only from their tombs what their proper names were. Children meanwhile were addressed as "Little Snot" or "Shithouse," or some such unattractive title, to avoid attracting the attention of jealous spirits. Moreover, the etiquette of conversation prohibited anything like cross-questioning; one or two questions in a row perhaps, never three. Consequently, it was impossible to collect a genealogy at one sitting. To figure out the connections between individuals was a painfully slow and fitful business.

The people I knew best were my immediate hosts, the government-appointed headman and his large family. For me to stay with them was the normal arrangement: travelers with no kin in the longhouse invariably stayed in the headman's apartment. This included Upriver People traveling to and from the shops and hospital at Marudi, as well as government officers, such as people from the District Office and agricultural extension workers. They, however, seldom lingered more than a few days, and it worried me that my long-term residence was an abuse of custom, and a drain on my host's resources. I tried to make appropriate gifts to pay my way, and I cast about for some other accommodation. The longhouse was, however, an old one, not rebuilt for a generation, and since there had been no opportunity to segment, each apartment was crowded with the married children and grandchildren of the founders. There were no empty rooms that I could use, and so for the moment I had to stay put.

After half a year, however, I was past the initial stages of adjustment, and beginning to fret that I was not active enough in pursuing my research goals – whatever my research goals were, for what I had written an age before in my grant application had long since gone out of focus. In my indecision, I aimed at targets of opportunity, collecting whatever I could with whoever would spend time with me. In that frame of mind, I discovered Tama Usang Weng, or he discovered me, for he was a man starved for conversation. Like old men elsewhere, he wanted to talk about his youth and the things he had seen and done, but most of his neighbors found his endless anecdotes boring, and laughed at him behind his back. I was as much a godsend to him as he was to me, though I often found him exhausting. He had been married at different times to women in several longhouse communities, and he would absent-mindedly switch back and forth between different languages. I was often totally lost, but my panic was reduced when I found that others sitting nearby were equally adrift. It was hard not to conspire with them with covert winks and nods, but I resisted the temptation. Unlikely as our relationship was, I felt a warmth towards him, and a loyalty of friendship.

Despite his earlier marriages, Weng had been married for many years to a woman called Tina Usang, that is, "Mother (*tina*) of Usang," the son whose father (*tama*) was Weng. My friend was sometimes referred to briefly as Tama Usang, sometimes more formally as Tama Usang Weng, and sometimes, somewhat disrespectfully, as Old Weng. After a while, I discovered that Tina Usang had been for many years a shaman of note, although she had given it up some years ago on account of her age. Tama Usang had played an essential part in her seances by playing special tunes for her on the *sapé*, a three-stringed wooden instrument, which had the effect of summoning her spirit helpers (see Figure 3). He also interpreted what advice the spirits, speaking through Tina Usang, had for those who came to her with problems, often illnesses in the family.

Figure 3 Tama Usang Weng playing the *sapé* that he used to accompany his wife when she was performing as a shaman. Photograph by author.

Several times they told me how much their services had been valued in the past. They became increasingly excited by their reminiscences, and, unknown to me, they resolved on a comeback. On the next occasion that a woman shaman performed in a neighboring room, Tina Usang got up and joined her.

Tina Usang's renewed activity as a shaman was judged a success, and people began to pay attention. It was remembered that she had been an adept in various shamanistic practices not recently seen. This came about, I later learned, because shamanism is prone to fashion. Supposedly, each shaman is individually inspired to perform in his or her own way, entirely idiosyncratically, but there were in fact styles characteristic of particular longhouses and periods. Tina Usang, having acquired her powers many years before, had a style so old-fashioned as to seem novel. People talked about the good old days when things had gone better in every way, and the excitement spread. A revival was planned, the climax of which was to be the construction of a mystical barrier against evil influences (*rèng*), all around the longhouse. It was to be erected by several shamans over several nights, led by Tina Usang, and it was represented by a physical barrier made out of creepers of various kinds collected from the jungle. The chosen creepers were covered with thorns, so that the result looked strikingly like a barbed-wire entanglement.

While preparations for the rite were in progress, I was suffering doubts about the sudden enthusiasm that my enquiries had triggered off. On the one hand, I had not asked anybody to do any of this, and it was not being done for my benefit. On the other hand, shamanism was thought to be a dangerous business; anything unexpected, any kind of shock Tina Usang experienced while her soul was away from her body on its astral journeys, could be fatal. She was frail. What if something went wrong? Would I be blamed?

In the end, I need not have worried, because Kasi had already made a decision. In the middle of the afternoon, when a small crowd was weaving the fence of thorns and preparing food offerings, she suddenly appeared. Drawing herself up to her full five feet two, every inch of her expressing resolution, she made a brief speech: people did not know what they were doing; *rèng* had not been made for many years; it was dangerous and unseemly to do it in a half-baked way; the proceedings would cease. No one demurred, and Kasi stalked off. The crowd dispersed, its enthusiasm deflated. Tama Usang shrugged, and only Tina Usang grumbled openly about Kasi's highhandedness. As for me, I felt mixed emotions. Her intervention had taken me completely by surprise, and I didn't understand it. At first I was relieved, but it wasn't long before I began to feel resentment. Unable to appreciate the reasons that Kasi had given, I took her actions personally. She had made it clear that I had no such prestige as that associated with the former colonial order that would prevent her from interfering with whatever plans I made. She had reduced my friends in my eyes, and me in theirs.

The polite fictions of research proposals

My confusion about Kasi was part of a more general uncertainty. It will come as no surprise to most anthropologists who have been through the experience that, six months into fieldwork, I was distressingly vague about what it was I was up to. Did that make my grant application a lie? Having found out that the project I had designed was neither practical nor relevant, was I operating under false pretenses in continuing to spend the money that I had been given? My funding, as it happened, came mostly from the Ford Foundation via an agency, now defunct, called the Foreign Area Fellowship Program. But I might as easily have received my major support from a government program, such as the National Science Foundation, and then I would have been dithering at taxpayers' expense. I might note that my funding was tiny compared to the sums spent on projects in other sciences, in total barely more than twelve thousand dollars, and that my day-to-day living expenses were minuscule, but that would be a quibble.[1]

In personal terms, what lay between me and my closely argued, carefully referenced project design was a whole new way of life. I had for months been completely absorbed with pressing practical problems: how to get about by river, where to stay, where to sleep, how to feed myself, how to get by without plumbing, how to start conversations and avoid offending people. My previous existence as a graduate student became remote and unreal. Moreover, throughout this stressful period, I had been constantly asked to explain myself, and what I was up to. For government officials, I trotted out my lines about research under the aegis of the Sarawak Museum, which was at the time the only research institution in the state. For longhouse people, however, this account was largely meaningless, and I came up with bromides about studying their way of life, and writing a book. The problem was that the more I repeated these half-truths, the more vacuous they became, and I found it harder and harder to remember what in heaven's name I was supposed to be doing.

I can also describe the process in cool professional terms. Preparing my grant had made me probe the existing literature purposefully, looking for productive issues. The literature was out of date and old-fashioned, however. Worse, it tended to lump together all the people of the interior, obscuring the ethnic complexities that I had been learning about ever since I arrived. My experiences traveling about the watershed of the Baram river made the inadaquacies of the old literature apparent. When I finally chose a place in which to settle down to intensive research, I inevitably picked a particular community, and not some abstractly "typical" longhouse, which does not exist. Once settled, I set about looking for a range of institutions related to rigid systems of social hierarchy that were described in the old literature, and had provided the focus of my research proposal. But, hard as I looked, I could not find them. Was I blind or stupid? Were my language skills so inadequate? It took me months to convince myself that the absence was real, and longer still to understand what it signified, of which more below. In the meantime, there was my proposed research on class systems knocked on the head, and nothing in its place.

What eventually resolved the dilemma was the discovery of an institution that I had not expected to find at all. It seems a mere detail, but it was a significant one. Practices of secondary treatment of the dead are classically associated with Borneo, and have been the subject of speculation for a century, but the well-known cases are all in Indonesian Borneo, far away to the south. What that meant ethnologically was only sorted out later (Metcalf 1976), but meanwhile the central place of elaborated mortuary rituals in Berawan culture became ever more obvious. Whether I began with social organization – families, factions, and leadership – or with cosmology – the gods and the ancestors, the meaning of life and death – always the discussion led back to the same place. Even talking about the weather, the very stuff of an Englishman's small talk, often led back to mortuary ritual, because the deaths of important people were expected to produce thunder, lightning, and torrential rains (Metcalf 1992: 148).

Moreover, the death rituals were at that time the subject of intense controversy. Since the 1950s, conversion to one or other version of Christianity had been gathering momentum in Upriver communities. During the 1960s an indigenous revivalist movement sought to compete with Christianity by promoting a universal cosmology focused on the female deity Bungan, and a radically simplified set of rituals in place of all the complexity and diversity of the old religions. For a while, Bungan was highly successful, even recovering converts from Christianity, but by the time of my fieldwork in the mid-1970s, it was losing ground. By then, Long Teru was the only community in Baram to have persisted in its old religion throughout, staunchly resisting both foreign and Bungan missionaries, and providing me with an opportunity not to be missed. At the same time, however, the old ways could hardly remain unchanged when every longhouse festival brought guests self-conscious about their new faiths, and every marriage outside the community brought on a crisis. Consequently, there was constant debate about what rituals should be retained, and what concessions could be made. Under these circumstances, I bowed to the inevitable and focused my research on ritual continuity and change, so confirming the old saw that ethnographers end up studying whatever their hosts want to talk about.

Kasi throws up her defenses

My new research interests set me off in fresh directions. With various companions, I traveled far and wide to see old graveyards, with their beautifully carved wooden tombs. These were made of durable ironwoods, immune to rot and termites, and even when the jungle had grown over them their massive supporting posts, soaring up into the canopy, remained impressive and evocative of ancient glory. My guides were proud to show them to me, because they embodied the history of their nation. I also accepted invitations to funerals in neighboring communities, and no one found that in the least odd since death rites constitute the largest of all longhouse festivals, opportunities to socialize uninhibitedly, eat and drink prodigiously, and initiate all kinds of new social interactions, including marriages.

There were many people whom I could usefully talk to about the death rites, but often I found myself referred back to Bilo Kasi as the expert. My encounter with her during the Tina Usang affair had hardly been auspicious, but that was perhaps an exception and best put behind me. So I made my prestations of *arak*, and sat at her feet as she told stories of the ancestors whose tombs I had seen. Nevertheless, I remained cautious and respectful, never quite sure what she thought of me. At times, she seemed to enjoy instructing me in how to behave properly upriver, and I learned that she had done the same thing a generation before for English colonial officers who visited Long Teru. Like other longhouse people, Kasi thought that the English were on the whole good-hearted, but unsophisticated. Their manners left much to be desired, and they needed to be told when to shed their shoes and how to move in a properly bowed posture about a veranda crowded with people seated on the floor. Uncorrected, Englishmen had a tendency to make people uneasy by striding about as if they were in the jungle, and standing over them in postures that implied a childish truculence. They were even known – horror of horrors! – to step *over* reclining people. Kasi was much concerned with breeding, and listening to her it was easy to see Long Teru as a refuge of civilization in a brutal world.

At these times, sitting in Kasi's room during the day while she dandled a grandchild on her knee, I saw her in a relaxed mood. She was most comfortable, however, with a circle of women of her own age who had grown up together in the longhouse. They enjoyed an easy familiarity born of an entire lifetime spent together, all idiosyncrasies known, all frictions long since resolved. Particularly when things were quiet in the longhouse, they could be found in one of the kitchens at the back, perhaps with a bottle of something. Together, they had a schoolgirlish mischievousness about them that belied their age. In this mood, there was absolutely nothing they would not talk about if they so chose. They would guffaw scurrilously about all manner of ancient quarrels and the foolishness of men living and dead, and when they were done teasing me, they were the best informants in the world.

Kasi's skills appeared best in domestic settings. She was not prominent in rituals, where men took the lead, for instance in prayer. In addition to her storytelling, Kasi was expert in the epics sung about heroes of the past, warriors who fought monsters and climbed to the heavens. In the early 1970s, she regularly held a crowd all night long, singing verse after verse, with her audience providing the chorus. Increasingly, however, she needed to be coaxed into a performance, and she made the excuse that her voice was too old and cracked. This did not prevent her, however, from producing with impressive verve and volume the praise songs customarily offered as a courtesy to visitors, along with a glass of *arak*, which had to be drunk down at one go, no heel taps.

Nevertheless, there was one ritual context in which Kasi was the acknowledged expert, one that was restricted to public and deadly serious occasions: the all-important death songs. If ritual was to be my new research topic, then mortuary rites would inevitably occupy a great deal of my attention, and at the sacred core of the mortuary rites were the death songs. Nothing else in the religion of Long Teru was hedged about by taboos as they were. To sing them when there was no corpse in the longhouse was to cause a death, since the ancestors, once alerted to the arrival of a new member, would ensure there was one. Even to hum their tunes was dangerous, and anyone who forgot themselves so far as to do so was quickly and angrily hushed. I recorded many hours of the death songs during funerals, but the tapes were impossible to transcribe. While the event was in progress, the handful of old people able to play a useful part in them were up all night long singing. It was hardly reasonable to expect them to sit with me during the day, and it would anyway have taken far longer than one day to transcribe a night's recordings. At other times, no one would countenance me playing the tapes, let alone listening to them with me, over and over, line by line.

The dilemma was sharp: the more I learned about the songs, the more central they became, and at the same time, the more impenetrable. In the end, daunted by the intractable problems involved in making full transcriptions, I settled on the lesser goal of obtaining detailed summaries of their contents. But, to my frustration, these also proved elusive. Whenever I pursued the topic, the people I usually relied on became embarrassed and evasive, and slowly, by hints and nods, I was made aware that I was dealing with more than forgetfulness, more even than fear of offending the ancestors. Gradually it emerged that Bilo Kasi had once again decided to intervene forcefully. She had flatly prohibited anyone from discussing the death songs with me. Kasi herself, masquerading as my chief informant, talked about the songs in vague generalities, laying smokescreens, deliberately misleading me.

The siege[2]

The realization that Bilo Kasi was obstructing my research initiated a long struggle. Her behavior seemed to me unreasonable, not because I expected to be trusted with sensitive information, but because I already possessed the power to provoke the ancestors if I wanted to, and everybody knew it. I had the songs themselves on tape, and no one had seemed bothered when I had made the recordings during several death rituals over a period of months. My reel-to-reel tape recorder – state of the art in that era – was bulky and conspicuous, and, moreover, I had played back segments of the songs for the crowd while the rites were still in progress. Meanwhile, everyone agreed that it was the songs themselves, those words and cadences, that were lethal; merely talking about their contents was by comparison relatively unthreatening. Kasi's prohibition was therefore not prompted by fear of what harm any indiscretion of mine might bring to the community. I decided to evade it.

My tactics were those of siege. Time was on my side because secrecy is hard to maintain in the close social environment of the longhouse. It would take a great deal of vigilance on Kasi's part to police casual conversations, and her attempts to do so would sooner or later cause resentment. Her authority was great, but not unquestioned, and in the quotidian democracy of the longhouse all I had to do was wait. In the meantime, I probed my adversary's defenses. I learned to slip in a question about the death songs here and there, whenever vaguely relevant, trying to catch people off-guard. When I secured a snippet of information, I would refer to it casually while talking to someone else, implying I knew more than I did. Sometimes I drew startled looks, but more often my allusion prompted new information easily enough. Then I nodded away knowingly, my pencil set aside casually, while concentrating hard, so as to remember what I was told.

I began to enjoy the espionage. I learned how much could be inferred from careful collation of what I already knew. From simply being present when songs were sung, I knew their names and proper order, which were prescribed and which optional, and how long they lasted. The key ones were not the longest. Without any translation, I could work out a great deal about metrical structure revealed by repetition of phrases, lines, and verses. One important song had a very simple repetitive structure. I knew which songs had a narrative form and which did not. Sometimes I could recognize a word or two, or a proper name. This was enough to suggest questions that I might slip into conversations, and even evasive answers often provided information if carefully considered. All in all it was a valuable exercise in the close reading of ritual and its indigenous exegesis, for which the language of sleuthing, of clues and leads and sources, provides an appropriate vocabulary.

This was the only time in my fieldwork when I was aware of trying to get information out of people that they did not want to give. In contrast to many places in the world, religion at Long Teru was not a matter of esoteric knowledge. People varied greatly in what they knew, but this was a matter of personal inclination, not restricted access. Generally speaking, anyone might learn any ritual skill who took the trouble to pay attention, imitate, and ask questions. Questions, however, had to be about how to perform rituals, not what they meant. Moreover, the enquirer had to chose whom to follow; nothing was more likely to provoke old people into heated discussion than an innocent question about the niceties of ritual. The only real secrets at Long Teru were family secrets, and I found them out without trying. They were invariably betrayed to me by someone with a grudge, even though I usually had no reason to be interested.

Not surprisingly, I had always asked questions in a way that set me apart from other inhabitants of Long Teru. For one thing, I was more relentless in pursuit of particular topics, and this was risky because any appearance of cross-questioning was offensive. I was sensitive to the laughter that my questions sometimes provoked, in case it marked irritation, but in fact it was not easy to impose very far on Upriver People. If they disliked the direction of a conversation, they would change the subject or just wander away. Usually their laughter indicated that I had asked a question that no one had ever heard asked before, and that was interesting. Usually I was asking questions that had no answers, as far as they were concerned, the sorts of questions only children ask. But just occasionally, by my shotgun technique, I caught them by surprise with a question that ought to have an answer, but no one could quite say what it was – a productive question. Very rarely, I had the satisfaction of knowing more than anyone expected. But mostly, of course, I was aware only of my own clumsy persistence.

In seeking to overcome Bilo Kasi's prohibition, I went one step further: I set out to exploit the tensions that divided the community. Direct confrontation with Kasi's authority was impossible, and if I was ever tempted to speak ill of her, I thought better of it. To do so would certainly have caused people to close ranks against so obvious an outsider. There remained the possibility of collusion: I could engineer for potential prohibition-evaders a situation of credible denial. My usual way of doing this was to imply that Kasi herself had already told me all about something – after all she was claiming to be my principal informant. That would entitle my covert ally to launch into his or her account, beginning emphatically "Well then, as you already know . . ." What convinces me that I engaged in these little farces on several occasions was the over-acting indulged in by both parties, talking away loudly for all to hear, while privately nodding away conspiratorially.

Clearly, by this stage in my fieldwork, a year and a half into it, I had enmeshed myself in a web of lies. Everyone – I, Kasi, my old and new allies – was misrepresenting his or her goals and intentions, in an ever-expanding web of deceit. Strangely enough, I was not entirely unhappy with this development. At the beginning of my fieldwork, I would have been completely incapable of such subtlety; and was it my imagination, or was I better liked by many people at Long Teru? They had often laughed with me about the English colonial officers who walked around the house smiling inanely, hardly able to say a thing. They found them too simple to be fully human. How much worse must I have looked when I first arrived? Now, their knowing, sideways glances seemed to say: you're catching on, finally. Is artful lying a measure of success in fieldwork? Is it indeed of what fieldwork technique consists?

My best informants were not at all the most gullible. Nor were they necessarily motivated by petty malice. As on other topics, some of my most reliable sources were the irrepressible old ladies who made up Kasi's own peer group, and with whom she enjoyed such easy relationships. They, after all, were the least likely of anyone in the longhouse to be intimidated by her, and they were ready to make up their own minds about what I should know and not know. One even volunteered to come down to the coast with me, where we could sit in a hotel room and play the tapes. What did she care, she asked, if the songs killed people down there? This possibility excited me for a while, but there were practical problems: how long was it reasonable to expect her to stay in that alien environment, and could I afford hotel prices? In the event, the project was vetoed by the woman's family, who wanted to know what would happen if the songs killed *her*. It is considered a great misfortune to die a long way from home, because corpses more than a few hours old cannot be brought into the longhouse, and are therefore denied proper funerals.

Nevertheless, in the midst of all these alarms and excursions, a general picture of the death songs was emerging. On the opening night of the festival, the ancestors were summoned *en masse* to the longhouse, initiating a season of dramatic liminal confusion, at once empowering and dangerous. Eight or ten nights later, the dead and the living were carefully disentangled. The former, with their new recruit, were sung back to the land of the dead, while the souls of the living were called home again, one by one, to make sure they had not left with the ancestors. On the intervening nights, songs could be chosen in more or less any order from a vast repertoire, including ones borrowed from neighboring communities and sung in different languages. Some were nothing more than games – though every bit as dreadfully sacred – playful competitions, for which the prize of victory was a glass of rice wine to be drunk at one go, and the penalty for failure was the same. Others again recounted myths, somewhat like the epic songs that Kasi sometimes sang to entertain people in the evenings, but, once again, reserved for death rituals. Of these narrative songs, the most important described the origin of the death rites and the songs themselves (Metcalf 1982: 207–32).

My fifth column

For months I had worked intermittently on the death songs, and I had stopped hoping for any major breakthrough. I had come to terms with what I could and could not achieve. But I had not reckoned with Tama Usang Weng, husband of the shaman whose plans to revive her skills and throw a spiritual barrier around Long Teru had been so abruptly terminated by Kasi. Tama Usang was, after Kasi, the most important singer of the death songs. He led some of the songs, although not the essential prescribed ones on the first and last nights of a festival, and, as it turned out, he had arrived at his own opinion of what I should know about them.

One afternoon Tama Usang came unexpectedly to see me in the one-room building that had been the final compromise regarding my living arrangements. It stood level with the veranda directly in front of the room of the headman, with whom I maintained formal residence. It looked like one of the storage sheds under the line of trees by the riverside, but enabled me to have my own cooking arrangements and not be a drain on the headman's stores. It also allowed me to have a table where I could sit with my notebooks and papers, so it was called *oppis Pita* (Peter's office, see Figure 4). It had been necessary because Long Teru was an old house, and crowded, with no spare rooms. Meanwhile status considerations made the headman unwilling to have me build on either end. Only newcomers would do that, poor immigrants from other communities, and the

Figure 4 *Oppis Pita*. Under the house is a twenty-horsepower outboard motor – at the time the only one in the village. The longhouse is behind, with its steeply pitched shingle roof. The stairs at right lead up to the apartment of the headman. Photograph by Michael Melai Usang.

headman was reluctant to set me in that light. The back of the long-house was reserved for kitchens, and that left only one option. From my point of view, it was a good compromise. I had a pleasant view of the river on one side, so I could see who was coming and going, and on the other a panorama of anything going on on the veranda. At night a glance told me who was sitting up late to socialize or watch a shaman in action.

By the same token, my "office" had little privacy, and Tama Usang began his visit by closing the door and windows as tightly as possible. This was odd behavior, but I had become accustomed to Tama Usang's idiosyncrasies and sudden enthusiasms. I assumed that he was trying to evade observation from the longhouse – little chance of that – but it was not the community of the living whose attentions he feared to draw on himself. He sat me down next to him in the darkest part of the room, and began to whisper in my ear. He had decided that since I planned to leave soon, the time had come to tell me all about the death songs. I had been looking forward to a nap, but this was too good an opportunity to miss. For hours through the heat of the day, cooped up in my airless room, Tama Usang talked on and on, barely allowing any interruptions, and I scribbled away. The longhouse slumbered, then roused itself to late afternoon tasks, and then bathing in the river, and then cooking the evening meal, and still Tama Usang talked on in his cracked whisper. Finally, at about eight in the evening, he decided that he was done, and demanded a drink for his pains. I was glad enough to give it and sat back to contemplate my amazing and exhausting day. But it was not over yet. Having downed a couple of stiff drinks, Tama Usang made me collect my notes and trail off with him to the room of Bilo Kasi. She received us with stiff formality, while Tama Usang called her bluff. Politely but firmly, Tama Usang said that he had told me what I needed to know in order to understand their old ways, and to set them down correctly for the people who came after. He did not want anyone saying that he had got it wrong or told lies, so now Kasi would hear me through and say whether it was right or not. And that is what she did, smiling thinly whenever I looked up from my notes. Only a couple of times did she interrupt to correct a small point while I stumbled along, prompted by Tama Usang. It was the early hours of the morning before it was done. Kasi had been outmaneuvered, and not by me.

3 Power

Absurd as it may seem, the technical jargon of anthropology provides no more precise a term to describe my relationship with Kasi than as an "informant." So bland a word has always made ethnographers uneasy; it sweeps far too much under the rug. This is problem enough, but, as it happens, the accident of a shared Latin root causes another: the unsettling confusion between our good-natured informant, cheerfully helping science forward, and the sinister figure of the informer. Anthropologists find themselves insisting on a sharp distinction, and wince when journalists use the terms interchangeably, for instance in police stories. Unfortunately, however, the journalists are in the right of it. The *Oxford English Dictionary* lists one meaning of informant as "one who gives information," but another as "one who lays an information against a person." For informer, it has the same two meanings. There is no escaping the fact that in English the terms are virtually synonymous. French, naturally, has more clarity: *informateur* is not *dénonciateur*.

What is unsettling about this is that informers act by betraying the weak to the strong. As Patrick O'Brian has one of his Irishmen say: "the character of an informer is more despised in our country than any other, is it not? Rightly so in my opinion. Though, indeed, the creatures swarm there" (1970: 109). Informers swarmed in nineteenth-century Ireland because there was constant resistance to a deeply resented colonial regime, and they were despised because poverty made treachery so fatally attractive. In the twentieth century, there were plenty of similar situations; what does it say about anthropology's role in the world if we cannot distinguish our informants from informers, even lexically? We can, however, distinguish, at least in theory, the informer from the liar. In a paradox that would have pleased Oscar Wilde, the informer tells the truth and is despised for it, whereas the liar cannot be accused of betraying anything.

Hearts and minds

Bilo Kasi might well have seen Tama Usang Weng as an informer, *dénonciateur*, precisely because, unlike her, he told me everything, without deception. What undermined that charge was that no one else seemed to understand clearly why Kasi had decided that telling about the death songs was a matter for *omertà* – a vow of silence – while telling about ancestors who went to the moon was not. That confusion surely explains why many people at Long Teru – and not just those with grudges – were willing to collude with me in subverting Kasi's prohibition. As noted above, Berawan religion is not esoteric and, generally speaking, people who want to know about something can learn if they want to take the trouble. At funerals all forms of games are prohibited, and there is little else to do but learn the death songs. Kasi's prohibition was unprecedented, and directed only at me.

Meanwhile, the brilliance of Weng's maneuver was that by confronting Kasi and announcing openly what he had done he refused the classification of traitor. It was a bitter moment for Kasi, not only because her authority had been flouted, but because she had failed to convince people, failed to make them see what she saw. But what did she see? If she could not give Weng the character of an informer, it remains an open question to what extent I represented what in Ireland was called synecdochically "the Castle" – Dublin Castle, seat of administration and symbol of alien hegemony. In Sarawak as in Ireland, truth was entangled in power.

The irony is that I found it then – and find it still – almost impossible to think of myself as empowered during fieldwork. There I was alone, an outsider, far from home or anything familiar. Even towards the end of my stay, when I had my little routines worked out and people were used to having me around, I never got over the trauma of my arrival and its intense sense of vulnerability. Moreover, I remained pathetically sensitive to my current standing in the community, which sometimes fluctuated wildly. There was a party at Long Teru who always resented my presence, and another who were as steadily approving, but the majority blew hot and cold according as I was seen as generous or unyielding, entertaining or intrusive, and it was exhausting to be permanently anxious about popularity ratings, like some second-rate politician.[1] Such stresses are almost inevitable in fieldwork, wherever its location, in great metropolises as much as in remote corners. Nevertheless, they are particularly inescapable in relatively closed communities, as is shown with devastating effect in Jean-Paul Dumont's classic account (1978) of his convoluted relations with the members of a small Panare band in Venezuela. I can only add, by way of special pleading, that the longhouse seemed designed for sudden, gossipy waves of enthusiasm or disapproval.

Occasionally, however, a passing remark made it plain that my hosts did not see matters in the same light. For instance, young men whom I knew well from shared evenings in the longhouse or casual fishing expeditions would sometimes ask me whether I had "had enough" of longhouse life yet. The Malay term they used was *puas*, which might be glossed as "satisfied," a comfortable sense of fullness after a meal perhaps, but in this context it had connotations of boredom. What they resented about me – not always or continually, but repeatedly – was my ability to leave whenever I chose. In the mid-1970s, enough schooling was available for young men to know about the wonders of a world outside Borneo, a world they would never see. There was an irreducible inequity in our relationship; I could choose when to come and go from that world.

The most compelling moment for me in Dumont's account is not to do with the trials of his arrival or travails in establishing "rapport" – all reported at length – but in a brief scene of departure near the end of the book. A handful of Panare ferry him to the nearest place where he can find road transport. They joke with him:

> "You will starve there; there is no tapir in your settlement." Andres had a different opinion: "The *tatto* will eat you." Miron added, "The jaguar, too." Domingo Flores saw a different fate altogether for me: "He is going to write about us, a lot of writing with all the pictures he took; bring it here, we want to see it." But Domingo Barrios fantasized differently: "My father is a big liar. He will screw a lot and make many bearded babies." We all laughed together, and it was the memory I wanted to keep of my companions. I got up and said *utey*, "I am going." And I left and walked swiftly to the Creole settlement without turning around for the last look I preferred not to take.
>
> (Dumont 1978: 198–9)

Dumont never returned. I have been back several times, but I was never again a regular part of longhouse life as I was at the end of my initial two years of fieldwork. I had been a resident, however odd; afterwards I was only a visitor. I have maintained contact with individuals who happen to have, intermittently, postal addresses, telephone numbers, or even email addresses, but these are tenuous links with people who have left the longhouse. Certainly as far as Kasi was concerned, I walked out of their lives in a manner even more abrupt than my arrival in the first place. I was often twitted by a Catholic missionary, a man whose company I enjoyed, who had spent decades in Sarawak: "You anthropologists, you don't stay long."

It is sometimes argued that such ruptures are a thing of the past, because cellular phones and international migration increasingly prevent any neat segregation of the research locale. In response to a rapidly changing global economy, many anthropologists are engaged in multi-sited research both at home and abroad, or with immigrants in the metropole (Georges 1990; Glick *et al.* 1992; Marcus 1995; Passaro 1997; Sutton and Chaney 1987). For them, "the field" may be no further away than a couple of subway stops, and no departure has the wrenching finality of Dumont's "I am going." It is an illusion, however, to imagine that what results is a seamless melding of lives in and out of the persona of the researcher. Instead, there is an endless procession of small ruptures – uptown/downtown – whose culmulative effect is, in my experience, at least as painful as Dumont's exit. I learned this in Auckland, New Zealand, which, because of unrestricted immigration from such formerly British possessions as the Cook Islands, Fiji, Samoa, and Tonga, not to mention immigration to the city by rural Maori, became in the 1960s the metropolis of the Polynesian people. Meanwhile students and faculty in Anthropology at Auckland University had access to only very meager research funds; willy-nilly they became pioneers in immigrant studies and multi-sited research (Hooper and Huntsman 1973; Macpherson 1976; Metge 1964; Salmond 1975). It is unfortunate that their work has been overlooked by American scholars now confronting similar circumstances. What I learned, as a mere undergraduate, was how difficult it was to conform one minute to Polynesian conversational styles and body language – or at least not stick out too much – and a moment later return to the modes of the university. It was the rare person who could manage the constant changing of masks without a jarring sense of falsity, and this applied even to academics who were themselves Polynesian.

Ethnographers pride themselves on the personal relations they forge in fieldwork, as contrasted to the superficiality of sociologists' surveys and questionnaires. There is nothing counterfeit in this; these relationships often provide desperately needed emotional support to the insecure researcher, and create a genuine bond with his or her hosts or companions. There is a second, less comfortable, reality, however, which is that all such relationships are to some extent exploitative. Does the second reality negate the first? One might argue that psychic needs of some kind or another underlie all human relations, but the peculiarity of friendships in fieldwork is that they bridge cultural boundaries that, almost invariably, also mark differential distributions of wealth and influence. Whatever the fieldwork circumstances, there is no escaping this. The moral ambiguities of fieldwork are only masked when such terms as "co-researcher" or "counterpart" are substituted for "informant." Some anthropologists like to speak of their fieldwork "mentors," reemphasizing just the allegory of student and teacher that we noted in the previous chapter. Another alternative, "fieldwork consultant," has ludicrous overtones of leather briefcases and flip charts. George Stocking comes closest to avoiding euphemism with his neutral phrase "ethnographic intermediaries" (1983: 10).

The relations of fieldworkers to their informants first became politicized during the Vietnam war. If it seems an unwarranted leap from the nuances of interpersonal relations to such a geopolitical crisis, the point is exactly that the relations between informant and fieldworker may be seen to reproduce in miniature the relation between colony and colonizer. In the case of Vietnam, what caused the one to become unmistakably implicated in the other was the early characterization of the war as a struggle for "hearts and minds." As Field Manual 31–16, Counterguerrilla Operations, stated:

> The vast majority of the population in any given target area is initially non-responsive and apathetic to either the aims of the indigenous government and what it stands for or the advocates of the revolution. The active advocates of revolutionary war constitute a very small but capable and active segment of the population. It is estimated that less than 10% of the total of the population has actively participated in or supported the initial efforts of the movement. Because of this the effort to influence the balance of the population is important.
>
> (Department of the Army 1962: no pagination)

The percentages sound rather like a US election, and what was needed were effective spin doctors to convey to Vietnamese peasants the American view of what the war was about. Under these circumstances, anthropologists with experience in southeast Asia were under pressure to become "ethnographic intermediaries" themselves.

Anthropologists have been involved in military affairs before, of course, the most celebrated case being Edward Evans-Pritchard's raising of irregular troops in the Sudan, where he had previously conducted fieldwork, in order to harry the Italian forces across the border in Ethiopia (Geertz 1988).[2] In much the same way, ethnic minorities in Vietnam had been recruited early in the war, following a pattern established by the French (Salemink 1991). Even at that stage, however, the deployment of the Green Berets signaled an ideological conception of the war unlike anything seen before. All college graduates with skills in foreign languages, the Green Berets were evidently seen by John Kennedy as a kind of Church Militant against communism, missionaries as much as soldiers. When Kennedy took office there were fewer than 700 advisors in Vietnam, but there were approximately 16,000 when he died (Barrett 1993: 14). This phase of the war began with an emphasis on "civic action," meaning development projects and education. Such projects proved impractical in an already war-torn country, however, and they were inconsistent with coexisting army doctrines that emphasized destruction of an enemy (Cable 1986: 111–57). American special forces found themselves in a war of assassination and counter-assassination in which any Vietnamese "informant" was liable to be a victim.

Meanwhile, graduate students in anthropology departments in the US were caught up in the maelstrom of antiwar resistance that began on college campuses. Struggling to distance themselves from any implication in the war, they took refuge in a kind of fiscal puritanism. The crucial moral precept was to avoid any taint of Defense Department funding in fieldwork. One scandal followed another, and paranoia spread well beyond Vietnam. In Thailand, the Hill Tribes Project was shown to have CIA connections, and in Sydney its Director, William Geddes, who had previously worked without controversy in Sarawak, was vilified by his own students (Geddes 1957). In vain did he protest that he did not know of the CIA connection, that he had never been pressured to do anything other than collect folklore, and that he never provided anyone with the names of informants. Similar controversy swirled around the Himalayan Border Countries Project (Berreman 1969), and in South America the ironically named Project Camelot became the most infamous of them all (Langer 1967). The Pentagon was interested in recruiting anthropologists wherever counterinsurgency warfare threatened, and that was a lot of the places where anthropologists worked.

It is surprising how rapidly that epoch has been forgotten. A generation later, graduate students do not seem unduly worried about where their funding originates, and they shock their teachers by even finding nothing particularly problematic about being supported overtly by the Defense Department, through such agencies as the National Security Education Program. With the Cold War a distant memory, Geddes' protestations of innocence would perhaps now be received more sympathetically, and indeed it is hard to explain how most of what anthropologists learn could possibly be bent to tactical use. How could the CIA have profited from knowing the contents of Berawan death songs, for instance? Moreover, my Berawan hosts were hardly in a position to know or care that my money came largely from the Ford Foundation and not the Pentagon. Nevertheless, it significantly framed my research that there was a communist insurgency in Sarawak in the 1970s that tied down a considerable part of the Malaysian army, mainly troops from West Malaysia. For one thing, I was taken at one point to be a communist agent, presumably because I stayed around a long time and lived modestly, but did not evangelize. It is interesting that having suspected that I might have another ideological agenda entirely from the missionaries, no one in the longhouse thought to turn me in to the security forces, which enjoyed scant popularity upriver. As it happened, there was no fighting in the particular area where I worked, but I could easily have imagined circumstances in which I would have been put in intense moral dilemmas had the case been otherwise. Finally, and at the risk of sounding like a prophet of doom, I do not think the world is so changed that anthropologists will no longer find themselves in the middle of wars for "hearts and minds," and then these issues will be as pressing as ever.

Colonial involvements

The Vietnam war heralded the current soul-searching in anthropology. The war was barely finished, however, before stern critiques began to appear from a new and unexpected quarter, namely literary criticism. Edward Said's *Orientalism* (1978) provided the opening salvo, arguing broadly that the West's perception of everything East of Suez, and reflexively of itself, was shaped by the political circumstances of their interaction, principally colonialism. Moreover, Western scholars were complicit in this process; far from resisting it, they had promoted it. Their representations of the Orient were inevitably "tinged and impressed with, violated by, the gross political fact" of colonialism (Said 1978: 11). Anthropology is included in this attack (1978: 2), but mostly by implication; Said's real interest, to which he returns in his later book *Culture and Imperialism* (1994), is in reading authors such as Joseph Conrad and Jane Austen in their global political context.

Anthropology is even more marginalized in Gayatri Spivak's elaboration of Said's argument, to which she adds the deconstructive philosophy of Jacques Derrida. Her essay "Can the Subaltern Speak?" ([1988] 1994) has achieved equal foundational status with *Orientalism* in postcolonial theory (Moore-Gilbert 1997),[3] and makes an even broader attack:

> We should also welcome all the information retrieval in these silenced areas that is taking place in anthropology, political

science, history and sociology. Yet the assumption and construction of a consciousness or subject sustains such work and
will, in the long run, cohere with the work of imperialist
subject-constitution, mingling epistemic violence with the
advancement of learning and civilization.

(Spivak 1994: 90)

I take this to mean, first, that anthropology may have a pat on the
head for its efforts over the years to pay attention to marginalized
people – tribals, peasants, and the like – who have no voice themselves in "learning and civilization." But, and here we drop the
other shoe, this "information retrieval," or fact-grubbing, function
betrays those same people by boxing them into Western notions,
particularly those of the individual, and so preparing them for an
equally mute place within the capitalist world system.

How to deal with such a charge? I do not doubt that Spivak points
to a real and present danger. If I try to understand Kasi's motives, do
I just make her into a replication of myself ("imperialist subject-
constitution")? Can I only re-present her by erasing what she really,
unknowably, is ("epistemic violence")? At the inception of anthropology in the late nineteenth century, Edward Burnett Tylor fell
directly into the trap by elevating "empathy" into a research
methodology (Burrows 1966: 240–51; Tylor 1964 [1878]). The
technique consisted of putting himself imaginatively in the place
of "primitive" people, so that he could work out the erroneous
deductions that lay behind their animistic religions. Tylor's projec-
tions are now ridiculed, but it is amazing how frequently the
hydra of psycho-reductionism rears its head anew. To presume,
however, to see into other people's minds immediately defeats our
purpose. It is only hesitantly that I can make out any part of
Kasi's world, but, as any storyteller knows, hesitations have their
dramatic impact. On this I have already taken my cue from Kasi:
they lie, we lie.

It is striking how similar to the critiques of Said and Spivak were
those made by anthropologists themselves. *Anthropology and the*

Colonial Encounter, edited by Talal Asad (1973), is a book whose impact has only grown over the years. Well before the rise of post-colonial theory, Asad argued: "It is because the powerful who support research expect the kind of understanding which will ultimately confirm them in their world that anthropology has not very easily turned to the production of radically subversive forms of understanding." Here is the issue of funding again, but phrased not in terms of the military establishment so much as "the establishment" in general; presumably it applied as readily to the Ford Foundation as to the CIA. This reveals the contrasting views from Britain, still in the 1970s obsessed by the process of "decolonization," and the US, where Vietnam filled everybody's vision. He continues: "It is because anthropological understanding is overwhelmingly objectified in European languages that it is most easily accommodated to the mode of life, and hence to the rationality, of the world power which the West represents" (Asad 1973: 17). His indictment prefigures Spivak's, shorn of philosophical jargon.

Moreover, Asad has equally caustic remarks to make on the day-to-day practice of anthropology, which lies beyond Spivak's view. He frames the relationships formed during fieldwork in this way:

> The colonial power structure made the object of anthropological study accessible and safe – because of it sustained physical proximity between the observing European and the living non-European became a practical possibility. It made possible the kind of human intimacy on which anthropological fieldwork is based, but ensured that that intimacy would be one-sided and provisional.
>
> (Asad 1973: 17)

In this passage, Asad puts his finger on a very practical reason for the chronological correlation between anthropology and colonialism. The New Guinea Highlands provides a particularly clear example; as "pacification" proceeded, so the anthropologists followed behind. Some daring souls followed very closely, moving into areas where Australian administration was recent and flimsy, but none moved ahead of the line of control. The process is fascinatingly documented in a collection edited by Terence Hays (1992). The very first into the Highlands was Reo Fortune, who arrived in the Finintegu area in 1935, but constant warfare forced him out only six months later. As Ann McLean shows (1992: 37–67), fieldwork was almost impossible, even for such a veteran as Fortune, who had already conducted his celebrated research in Dobu, Manus, and the Sepik. Shortly after Fortune left, the whole region was declared "uncontrolled" and nonadminstrative personnel were banned from entering.

Other essays in *Anthropology and the Colonial Encounter*, however, add nuance to the simple correlation by exploring ethnographically the relations of anthropologists to particular colonial regimes. Wendy James shows that those in the African colonies who fancied themselves as "practical men" usually saw anthropology either as quaint – concerned with folklore and antiquities – or as meddling in affairs it knew nothing about. A certain P.E. Mitchell, provincial commissioner in Tanganyika, thought that circumstances demanded something akin to a "general practitioner" rather than a laboratory specialist, someone who could take care of such things as cultural misunderstandings between African laborers and their European bosses (James 1973: 53–5). One is relieved that he found none such available in Africa; evidently anthropologists never became the handmaidens of colonialism to that extent. Richard Brown describes the controversy and antagonism that surrounded the Rhodes–Livingstone Institute. A progressive governor coerced mining companies into supporting the Institute, but they vehemently opposed Godfrey Wilson's plans for research in their own labor lines, on the curious grounds that it would involve "fraternizing" with Africans. They also feared outside "agitation" of otherwise contented African workers (Brown 1973: 181–93). As James concludes, if anthropology was, in Kathleen Gough's famous phrase, "the child of Western imperialism" (1968: 403), it was indeed "a problem child" (James 1973: 43).

Going into the villages

The critiques of anthropology's colonial involvement presume the discipline in its modern form. With the possible exception of Said, no one is much concerned with the professional practice of nineteenth-century "armchair" anthropologists. Between the two lay an intermediate generation who at least traveled abroad, making full use of the colonial infrastructure to practice a kind of "veranda anthropology." The shift to fully modern methods occurs, conventionally, between the fieldwork of A.R. Radcliffe-Brown in the Andaman Islands in 1908–9 and Bronislaw Malinowski in the Trobriands in 1915–17 (Kuper 1973: 37; Stocking 1983; Young 1979: 4–20). As Malinowski famously advocated:

> . . . the anthropologist must relinquish his comfortable position on the veranda of the missionary compound, Government station, or planter's bungalow, where, armed with a pencil and notebook and at times a whisky and soda, he has been accustomed to collect statements from informants . . .
>
> (Malinowski 1954: 146–7)

It is characteristic of veranda anthropology that we seldom know who these informants were who were summoned out of their villages, perched on unaccustomed straight-backed chairs, and cross-questioned through an interpreter. We can make a reasonable guess, however: it would have been people known to the missionary, the district officer, or the planter; most likely the village chief or headman – someone already familiar with role of intermediary, with *representing* his fellow villagers. It might have been an elder, but not anyone who much resembled Muchona. The British policy of Indirect Rule made this all the more likely, since colonial administration was conceived as a hierarchy that led from British officials, through indigenous authorities, down to the village. "First find your chief," advised Lord Lugard, originator of the policy, and it is likely that Radcliffe-Brown followed his advice

(Lloyd 1984: 272–3). Presumably, women were not often subject to this grilling, because they did not figure in the hierarchy. Moreover, who knows what sexual connotations there might have been in summoning them alone to the district officer's bungalow, let alone the planter's (Stoler 1991)?

Everything about the informant-on-the-veranda points to his subjugation. However, recent attention to modes of indigenous resistance (Scott 1984; Scott and Kerkvleit 1986) makes us pause to question just how docile he in fact was. James Scott's list of the "*ordinary* weapons of relatively powerless groups" includes several that might have been mobilized effectively against the anthropologist: "footdragging, dissimulation, false-compliance, pilfering, feigned ignorance, slander, arson, sabotage" (Scott 1986: 6, italics in the original). If the informant had the opportunity, he also had any number of motives. He might seek to inflate his own standing in the local community, enshrining it in a spurious ancient lineage, and in the process denigrate his rivals. Having gained the ear of the colonial authorities, he might use their backing to impose the kind of preeminence about which he had originally fantasized. Alternatively, he might have less self-interested motives, trying instead to turn the attention of his interrogators away from practices that had caused friction with the authorities in the past. According as he understood the predilections of his hearers, he might bowdlerize traditional rituals, or suppress references to magic or shamanism – the possibilities are endless.[4]

It was of course to escape these limitations that anthropologists followed Malinowski's advice to "go into the villages" (1954: 147), and it is clear that he thought the change in practice was revolutionary, bringing about a complete break with the past. A major aspect of this was behavioral: it made all the difference in the world that ethnographers in future would watch with their own eyes what went on "in the villages," and even at times join in – the celebrated "participant observation."

In the business of recruiting informants, however, it is not clear that the break was so radical. Let us observe Victor Turner, for example, on his way "into the villages," and towards his encounter with Muchona. He arrived in Lusaka, capital of what was then Northern Rhodesia (now Zambia), towards the end of 1950, and made the necessary round of visits in order to introduce himself to colonial officials and the staff of the Rhodes–Livingstone Institute (now the Institute for African Research), particularly its director, Clyde Mitchell. In December he went by road to the tiny administrative center of Mwinilunga Boma in the far northwestern corner of the country, where he stayed in the government "resthouse," that is, the bungalow reserved for transient British civil servants. He arrived in time to spend Christmas with the District Commissioner, Richard Dening. It was there that he first met someone who was to be crucial in his fieldwork, Musona, who often appears in Vic's writing under the pseudonym "Kasonda." (Beware: the similarity of the names Musona and Muchona may cause confusion. They were two very different people.) Musona was the caretaker of the rest house, and he spoke good English. Vic lost no time in making friends, so that when he moved on he took Musona along. Musona rapidly became indispensable as guide, translator, and general factotum (see Figure 5).

This pattern of recruiting as general helper someone met very early on in fieldwork is surprisingly common. The advantages for Vic are obvious; Musona knew his way around, and he could be useful before Vic had learned any Ndembu at all. What Musona had to gain is less obvious, but it is not hard to guess. At the very least, he improved his status from that of a janitor, and put his language skills in English to work profitably. He also got to travel around the countryside, and Vic undoubtedly provided him with a real opportunity to broaden his experience. What we should note, however, is the way the colonial infrastructure predestined their relationship.

My variation on this pattern was to seek out boarding students at the government secondary school in the small town of Marudi, many of whom came from longhouses in the interior. They lived spartan lives in the crowded dormitories since their parents could

Figure 5 Musona (third from left, looking away) at rite of *isoma*, for procreative problems. Photograph courtesy of the Turner Archive.

seldom provide them with anything more than a rice allowance. Consequently, for the treat of a meal in the bazaar they would happily talk to me for hours, and it was amazing how much they knew about the interior. Every vacation, they had to make their way home on the cheap, however far away was their native community. They had been everywhere, and seen everything. Moreover, they all spoke English, which was in those days the medium of instruction. The first language skill I acquired in Borneo was the variety of English spoken by high school children in Sarawak, and it stood me in good stead in dealing with government officials, because they had all acquired the same accent under the same circumstances. It would not be an overstatement to say that the friends I made at that time had more influence on shaping my subsequent fieldwork than anybody else, and I should mention in particular George Jenggang of Long Jegan with whom I first visited Berawan longhouses. Later, after I settled at Long Teru, I hired a recent graduate from the Catholic mission school in Marudi, Michael Melai Usang, initially to help me work on language skills. (Note that Berawan often share the same name without implying kinship connections. Weng, father of Usang, was no relation of Melai, son of Usang, christened Michael.) He was a popular young man, embodying the Berawan virtues of vigor and decisiveness and evidently destined to become a leader of the community. Throughout my fieldwork he smoothed the path for me in many ways, and gave invaluable help particularly with transcribing tape recordings. He was, however, a Christian enthusiast, so before long I had also to distance myself from him.

After some weeks, Dening introduced Turner to Chief Ikelenge, whose village was some forty miles to the north. Turner makes it clear (1957: 8–14) that Chief Ikelenge's authority had little traditional basis, and his administrative functions were largely a creation of the colonial government. Nevertheless, he maintained an establishment of his own, with an office staff and messengers. He was the superior of other local chiefs, and he maintained a tense relationship with the ritual leader – theoretically his superior – who bore the

Figure 6 Chief Ikelenge (wearing tie) with his staff in front of his offices at Mwinilunga. Seated to the right are three sub-chiefs, and on the left his ritual superior, the Kanongesha. Photograph courtesy of the Turner Archive.

title Kanongesha (see Figure 6). Edie Turner, who, with three small children, joined her husband in January 1951, was suspicious of Chief Ikelenge's ambitions, as apparently were many Ndembu. For a time, however, he played a central role in facilitating the Turners' fieldwork (see Figure 7). Since there was no resthouse at Chief Ikelenge's compound, the Turners briefly occupied a house owned by the fundamentalist Christian Mission to Many Lands, but they soon moved to their own "camp" at a spot chosen because it provided easy access to several villages by road. The camp consisted of a "grass" house, such as people in the region used on hunting trips, plus a couple of tents, but Edie recalls that anyway life was largely lived out of doors. Their usual modus operandi at this stage was to visit villages whenever there was a ritual in progress, using their diminutive Austin pickup truck, and return to camp to write up fieldnotes. In February 1952, they left for mid-fieldwork leave in Capetown and Manchester.

They returned to Mwinilunga District in May 1953, and established a new base at Kajima, which in Turner's ethnography is given the pseudonym "Mukanza." Kajima was Musona's home village, and his mother's brother was headman there. Their "camp" first consisted of two tents in the middle of the village. Later it was more luxurious, with several grass houses and a bell tent, pitched just outside the circle of houses that made up the village (see Figure 8). Here is how Edie Turner describes life in Kajima:

> We lived in the center of Kajima village along with nine related families, who entered our lives more and more. At night we heard Musona shouting from within his house to his older sister Manyosa within her hut two doors away, and we could hear Manyosa's indignant counter remarks. This village was like one great house owned by one extended family, with the sky roofing its minor units. . . . The odd circle of huts seemed to parade around the shelter in the center of the plaza. The shelter was the men's meeting place, in a sense, their pub; it was called the chota, a much used word. It was merely a wide

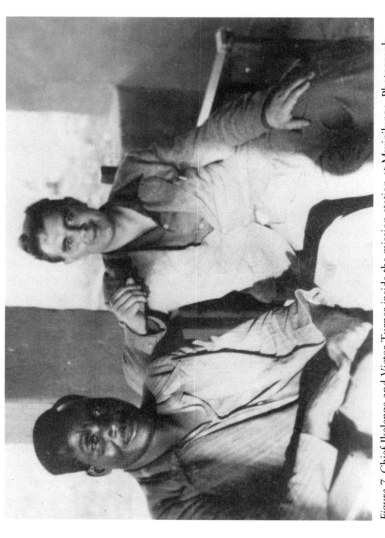

Figure 7 Chief Ikelenge and Victor Turner inside the mission station at Mwinilunga. Photograph courtesy of the Turner Archive.

cone of thatch, a round straw hat set on posts with a log fire inside and, to sit on, a log or two, an ancient deck chair, and an African stool for the headman. You could smell the soot in the old thatch; the posts were dark and rubbed shiny. Inside the buzz of conversation never ceased. . . .

(Edith Turner 1987: 15)

On the map of "Mukanza" opposite page 35 of *Schism and Continuity* (Turner, 1957), their camp would have been located in the top right corner, approximately where the box is marked "KEY." It was during their stay at Kajima that the Turners did their most productive work, but not all their data came from Kajima. They continued to travel, but not by van; their Austin pickup broke down shortly after they arrived in Kajima and was not repaired. Turner's long account of "Mukanda: The Rite of Circumcision" (1967: 151–279), for instance, was the result of an extended visit to a village a day's travel on foot to the south. Musona continued to be guide and translator.

The move to Kajima made Musona more central to the Turners' fieldwork than ever, but it was only a few weeks later that Vic met Muchona. Edie Turner remembers that the two rapidly became rivals for Vic's attention, and Musona bitterly resented being left out of the "seminars" with Muchona and the local schoolteacher Windson Kashinakaji. Meanwhile, it was Musona who was well connected in local politics. Since his mother's brother was headman he was in a strong position to inherit the role by matrilineal succession, and when Edie returned in the 1980s she found that he had indeed done so. Muchona, on the other hand, was not at all well placed socially, so he had taken the other route to authority via ritual expertise, and Edie discovered that Muchona's son in due course followed the same path, becoming an elder in a fundamentalist Christian church.

I narrate these details to show the ongoing connection with colonial infrastructure in a classic piece of fieldwork from the 1950s. It hardly needs saying that the Turners produced ethnography of a

Figure 8 View from the Turners' "camp" at Kajima. In front are two of their tents and their Austin pickup truck, and in the mid-distance the men's meeting place, or *chota*. Photograph courtesy of the

depth that went far beyond anything produced by "veranda anthropology," so much so, in fact, that Edmund Leach took it as a sign of theoretical retreat. In his influential essay *Rethinking Anthropology*, first presented as a Malinowski Memorial Lecture just two years after the appearance of Vic's *Schism and Continuity*, Leach complains: "Most of my colleagues are giving up the attempt to make comparative generalisations; instead they have begun to write impeccably detailed historical ethnographies of particular peoples" (1961: 1). Just beginning his stormy love affair with French structuralism, Leach was looking in the wrong direction to notice the beginnings of the British strand of symbolic anthropology. Turner's work soon became as influential as Leach's, and richness of ethnographic detail did nothing to impede that progress. On the contrary, it provided a vindication of Malinowski's program – but note the modulated descent from the veranda into the village, through a stage of visiting from a base camp. It is not as direct a journey as Malinowski implied. There is also the same movement in the choice of informants; a gradual venturing out from under the colonial umbrella.

In the postcolonial era, these circumstances might be taken as an historical curiosity, but that was not my experience. Even though I worked in Sarawak more than a decade after independence, my path "into the villages" had real similarities to the Turners'. If anything, I was even more concerned with government administrators, since I had always to worry about my visa status. For the Turners, having the backing of established academics at home and a local research institution meant that they could be confident of their ability to conduct their research. I did not enjoy the same luxury. When Sarawak joined the Federation of Malaysia in 1962, one condition was that Sarawak would retain control of its own immigration policy. Consequently, I needed research clearance from both Kuala Lumpur and Kuching, and it was said in the early 1970s that if one approved, the other automatically would not. Meanwhile, any slight diplomatic contretemps between Malaysia and the US would cause cancellation of all research visas. Sarawak has been closed to research for extended periods since independence. Consequently, I worked hard in my visa application to be as inoffensive as possible, which meant double-guessing what issues were currently sensitive in Sarawak. This adds another dimension to the questions explored in Chapter 2 about the little lies that grant applications tell. Having finally received clearance, I spent more time than Victor Turner had in working my way through official channels, first in Kuching, administrative capital of Sarawak, and then the divisional headquarters in the coastal town of Miri. It was some weeks before I arrived in the tiny upriver bazaar town of Marudi, and presented myself to the District Officer for Baram. He had little to offer me, being new to the district, so after that I kept a low profile, reckoning that out of sight was out of mind.

This part of my narrative can be replicated, *mutatis mutandis*, by a great number of anthropologists working in places where fieldwork is politically sensitive and government approval necessary. That applies to North Americans or Europeans working just about anywhere in Asia, Africa, or South America – most of the world, that is. It will also have resonance for, say, a Japanese or Indian anthropologist working in Indonesia or Egypt. There is, however, a great deal of current research to which these constraints do not directly apply, for a US citizen working in the US, for instance, or anyone in their own country. About those cases it is not easy to generalize, but I would not be surprised to find that there are similar, perhaps more subtle, processes of becoming identified with, or beholden to, various agencies of authority.

My next set of practical problems had to do with transportation, and I solved them with the help of both government agents and missionaries. Unlike the Turners, I was dealing with a region of extreme ethnic fragmentation about which I had inadequate information, so I needed to travel around and find out who lived where, and that meant river travel. Meanwhile, the massive canoes were few and far between that could travel up through the rapids, driven by one or two outboard motors. I hitched rides where I could, and that usually meant either the canoes that brought passengers and supplies to the two or three Catholic mission stations, or those used by the malaria eradication teams. Both of these institutions brought me in touch with people who knew the region intimately, and I profited enormously from their knowledge. The malaria eradication teams kept maps showing the location of every occupied house, so that they could be sure to spray their walls regularly with DDT. Moreover, at every village I visited, I stayed in the longhouse apartment of the headman, as do all travelers on the river, official or otherwise. These men told me about their own communities and their neighbors, or found me people who could. Most were helpful and friendly, so that I felt as comfortable upriver as the Turners did in Mwinilunga District. Indeed, at that stage things had not much changed upriver from the recent colonial era.

When, the survey completed, I chose a community in which to work intensively, I once again dealt with a government-appointed headman. I formally asked permission to stay in his longhouse, but the request was somewhat empty since I was already his guest. As travelers routinely do, I was staying in his family apartment within the longhouse. Only those with kinship connections in the community would stay in any other room. Moreover, there could be no question of "camping" as the Turners had done, not in that swampy, mosquito-ridden jungle. That would have made me seem very odd indeed to people who think it uncivilized to live anywhere but in a longhouse. Inevitably, then, I stayed on month after month in the headman's room, exploiting his hospitality beyond anything that custom envisaged. It also meant that I knew the family better than anyone else in the longhouse. Without any conscious choice on my part, I had firmly associated myself with a particular faction within the longhouse, and it was not Kasi's faction.

Having summarized these circumstances, the question can now be put: if Kasi saw me as somehow representing "the Castle," what castle exactly would that have been? Like the Turners, I had extensively utilized a superimposed administrative infrastructure to gain access to an indigenous community. What I knew about that community I learned mostly from agents of that administration, and even in the village itself I was associated with the government's local appointee. Neither I nor the Turners struggled much to evade this path "into the villages," even if we had wanted to. Nevertheless, there was a difference: I had worked through a colonial-like administration in which the District Officer was not an Englishman but a Malaysian, and that complicated people's perception of me. Was I to be associated with the goals and methods of the new regime, in theory anticolonial but in practice neocolonial, or with its predecessor? My face suggested one thing, my associations another. Whether I was sitting in a government office or a longhouse apartment – although for very different reasons – the balance of trust and suspicion would shift back and forth in different contexts. Moreover, it was not even that simple, because there had been two previous regimes. The first was the private Raj of a dynasty of English adventurers, the famous White Rajahs of Sarawak, who drew their title originally from the Sultan of Brunei. The second was the direct British colonial rule put in place after the chaos of the Second World War (Reece 1982). Again, my face suggested at least a cultural background within Christianity, as opposed to Islam, which is the established religion of Malaysia; more room for trust or suspicion. Upriver, I had traveled in missionary canoes, but dissociated myself from missionary activities, or even spoken against them. Did that mean I was a communist – that alternative enshrined orthodoxy of Western culture? Finally, in the longhouse I had, in total ignorance, chosen sides in a tense stand-off that had lasted generations.

My point is this: the hackneyed charge that anthropology has been the handmaiden of colonialism is not so much wrong as undiscriminating. Certainly the intimate connection is there, but what exactly are its implications? At different times Kasi could and did treat me as representing the Malaysian government that was responsible for current conditions; the British Raj that had abandoned them to those conditions, and the Rajah who had betrayed them before that; the Catholic missionaries who sought to eradicate her culture and religion, or some vague modernity (secular humanism, the left) that produced the same result; and finally her political rivals in the longhouse, who were anyway in league with the first item on this list. Veering between outrage and nostalgia, Kasi constructed a whole galaxy of powers, and how I fitted into it was neither easy to say nor permanent.

All of this, however, leaves out of the picture another complicating factor: the source of Kasi's own authority. Here the comparison with Muchona is particularly revealing.

People invisible to the state

One of the things that made Muchona exceptional was that he appeared without any kind of introduction, almost as if he willed it himself. As Victor Turner describes it, the meeting occurred not in a township or village, not in the midst of a gathering or ritual, but as both happened to be walking "on a dusty motor road of packed red clay" (1967: 131) – about as liminal a space as one could imagine in Ndembuland. Moreover, Muchona lived in "a couple of low huts" beside the road, rather than within a village, but he was anyway a restless man. He frequently traveled about the District, attending rituals. He was rootless in Ndembu society because his mother had been a slave, "taken by the Ndembu before British rule was established" (1967: 134). This meant that he could not assemble around himself a core of matrilineal kin, as other leaders did in founding villages. To make things worse for Muchona, his mother had been transferred between villages as a debt slave. Muchona had evidently bought his own freedom, and had lived in the villages of several successive wives. His chances of attaining respectability, let alone leadership, were slim.

Turner attributed Muchona's ritual authority precisely to this liminal quality. It was the source of

> his great ability to compare and generalize. Living as he had done on the margins of many structured groups and not being

a member of any particular group, his loyalties could not be narrowly partisan, and his sympathies were broader than most of his fellow tribesmen. His experience had been richer and more varied. . . .

(1967: 134)

In his lifestyle, traveling here and there to attend rituals, Muchona of course resembled no one so much as Vic himself. Consequently, Turner's admiration for Muchona also serves as a justification not only for himself, but for the abilities of ethnographers everywhere to "compare and generalize" by virtue of being outsiders – an important premise of symbolic anthropology.

There is also an element of identification in Muchona's pathetic vulnerability. Vic describes how easily Muchona was bullied by established elders, who were suspicious of his closeness to Turner. Village gossip accused Muchona of giving away their secrets, or teaching witchcraft. On one occasion, Muchona appeared in a smart suit cut from white cotton cloth and purchased with cash he had received from Turner. This presumption above his station made villagers jealous:

Sure enough a few days later Muchona came to us in his usual khaki rags, looking utterly woebegone. "What on earth's the matter?" I asked. He replied, "This is the last time we can speak about custom together. Can't you hear the people talking angrily in the shelter?"

(1967: 148)

Given what Edie Turner reports about the rivalry between Muchona and Musona, it seems likely that the latter was behind this whispering campaign against Muchona. Vic succeeded, however, in smoothing over their differences, and he had of course the power of the colonial government behind him to defend him from any serious accusations of wrongdoing himself. Meanwhile, Muchona's liminality is emphasized in this episode, and he appears almost as a clown inversion of the ethnographer, even to dressing up in the ethnographer's clothes.

Muchona was invisible to the apparatus of the state, and that is why the Turners found him – or he found them – only late in their fieldwork. The same was true of my encounter with Kasi; I was not directed to her by anyone at the District Office, nor, for good reason, was she known to any of the missionaries. But there the resemblance ends. Rather than occupying a liminal position in her community, she was at its very center. Far from being bullied, she was, from my point of view, likely to do the bullying. I did, on occasion, give Kasi clothing, but they were not Western clothes. They were the sort of gifts that change hands at elite rituals: sarongs woven with a gold thread.

What, then, was the source of Kasi's authority at Long Teru? The question has several answers, but the first relates to a period in the 1940s when she had not been at all invisible outside Long Teru because she was married to the community's last widely influential leader: Penghulu (Government-appointed Chief) Lawai. Lawai was by all accounts a remarkable man. Widely admired for his diplomacy and easy sense of command, he was appointed Chief at a young age. His territory covered a whole tributary of the Baram river containing more than twenty communities, and he held the post until his early death. He traveled widely, both alone and with government officers. He also frequently entertained parties of visiting dignitaries at Long Teru, and there is a photographic record of these visits. Figure 9 is taken from a collection of photographs published by Hedda Morrison in 1957. It shows a banquet for an unidentified group of visitors, including another Penghulu and at least four Europeans. The food is spread out on a line of plates running the length of the veranda, just as at a major longhouse festival, such as the culminating feast of a mortuary ritual. The guests are in the place of honor, on the outside of the veranda, opposite the Penghulu's room. A second photograph from the same occasion shows the entertainment that would have gone on far into the night, comprising drinking and dancing. Morrison, no doubt thinking

Figure 9 Penghulu Lawai (on left in rattan cap) entertains officers of the Raj to dinner. Photograph by Hedda Morrison, courtesy of Alistair Morrison and the Echols Collection, Division of Rare and Manuscript Collections, Cornell University Library.

about the market for her book, chooses to show an attractive bare-breasted woman, suggesting a kind of *risqué* floor show, but this is misleading. In fact, everybody would have danced, children and old people included. Moreover, the guests themselves would be required to get up and imitate the extremely muscular male version of the solo dancing, and no one would have hesitated to laugh at the usually pathetic attempts of the Europeans.

In extending Long Teru's hospitality, Kasi was never inconspicuous. One of her skills was the special genre of song welcoming individual guests, filled with extravagant compliments couched in poetical language. At the end of the song, the guest was required to down at one gulp a large tumbler of the potent distilled liquor made from rice wine, to the cheers of the crowd. If he failed to do so, Kasi would not scruple to insist. Assisted by the young girls, she might even pin the unwilling guest to the floor, hold his nose till he opened his mouth, and pour in the liquor.[5] Long Teru hospitality was not to be refused, and such episodes were worth an hour of delighted hilarity.

Lawai was popular with British officials because he was a firm supporter of their policies for "progress" in the region, including improved access to medicine and schooling. In this he followed the lead of his predeccessor Orang Kaya Luwak, who in the 1890s had identified the Long Teru community with the colonial order, making their longhouse a frequent stopover for administrators traveling up the Tinjar. The last District Officer before the Japanese occupation came frequently to Long Teru because he liked to visit a large lake inland from the longhouse, where, as Berawan told it in the 1970s, he went fly fishing wearing a deer-stalker hat – evidently trying to pretend he was on a Scottish loch. Sometimes he brought a friend who was manager of the Burns Phelp Trading Company in Miri, and there are many anecdotes of the antics of these two at Long Teru.[6]

Lawai's urbanity with colonial officers was consequently the fruit of years of familiarity. There were strong leaders at Long Teru after him, but none achieved his eminence. Some years after his death, Kasi remarried. She chose a prominent man from another Berawan village who had himself served with distinction as an Upriver Agent, that is, an indigenous representative of the Raj operating from his own minuscule administrative headquarters. Having done so, she might have changed her teknonym. There were several others she might have taken, such as Mother (Tina) of X or Grandmother

Figure 10 A studio portrait of Penghulu Lawai and family. Kasi at right. Photograph by unknown traveling photographer.

(Sadi) of Y. Kasi chose, however, to remain Bilo Kasi; she has been the Widow Kasi for thirty years.

There is a studio portrait of Kasi and Lawai taken at Marudi in the 1950s.[7] It is preserved in the longhouse as an heirloom, and it shows a handsome couple (see Figure 10). Lawai sits, leaning slightly forward with a knowing air. On either side of him are his daughters, aged about six and ten, one dour, the other coquettish. Kasi stands a little apart, erect, shoulders squared, feet together, arms at her side – almost at attention, except there is nothing of the stiffness of a soldier about her. She wears nothing but a plain sarong, folded in front and hitched up so as to be modestly unrevealing. Her breeding is revealed, however, in earlobes that reach to her shoulders, stretched since she was a girl with heavy brass earrings. Her outfit is completed by a pair of simple bracelets and a necklace of ancient glass beads, which, of all heirloom property, are the most closely linked to prestige. Her hair is drawn severely back, and her eyebrows plucked, so that her face has the blank look of the genuine aristocrat. Her features are regular, more elegant than pretty, and she looks straight at the camera, uncompromisingly.

Lawai's self-presentation is a little more complicated. He is wearing a neatly pressed shirt and shorts, like a government officer. His hair is cut in English style, a radical departure at a time when most Upriver men adhered to the traditional shaved brows and long pigtail. Behind him hang the flag of Sarawak (the old Rajah's flag) and the Union Jack. At the same time, he is barefoot, as no English official in a similar situation would have been. This does not mean that he arrived at the studio without shoes, only that he observed Upriver etiquette in removing them when he stepped on the rattan mat (*lapit*) that can be seen in the picture. Nevertheless, he has the broad feet of a man who often goes barefoot; no doubt he wore leather sandals to the studio (nowadays they would be plastic). More significantly, he has round the tops of his calves the rattan bands that are associated with warriors, and peeking out from his shirt are the all-important beads.

The suitability of the match between Kasi and Lawai, the attractiveness of the young couple, and the prestige that Lawai brought to Long Teru gave their marriage the aura of a golden age, a Berawan Camelot. The real warmth of their relationship is hidden by the posed formality of the photograph, but it was not without its stormy episodes, according to village gossip. Kasi could be demure, when occasion required, but she could also be willful and outspoken, sometimes to her husband's embarrassment. Nor, it was whispered, had she always been strictly faithful.

I saw Kasi in all of these moods. On one occasion, I had a lecture from her about the proper deportment of girls in her day; how she had been taught to sit, stand, and walk modestly in the short kilts (*ta'a*) that were the traditional women's wear until replaced by the simple cotton sarong in the 1940s. *Ta'a* were made of heavy fabric, and often weighted down with old coins sewn on at the hem, but even so they provided a stern test of proper deportment. Kasi seemed sometimes to enjoy instructing me in proper Upriver ways, as if I was one of the young English colonial officers whose attention and respect she had once so easily commanded. At other times, however, she seemed impatient, associating me only with a dull modernity in which she had no place. I think, in the end, I disappointed her. I did not at all cut the bold heroic figure that those legendary District Officers had done. Had she known of Marx's bitter comment on Napoleon III at the beginning of *The 18th Brumaire*, to the effect that history occurs first as tragedy and then as farce, she might readily have included me in the second phase.

4 Ethnicity

No one at Long Teru ever forgot that the Widow Kasi had been married to Penghulu Lawai. That was not, however, the only source of her authority, or even the major source. What distinguished Kasi more than anything else was her acknowledged status as heiress to the Lelak tradition. That said, I need to explain the significance of Lelakness, and in doing so I open a Pandora's box of complications and qualifications about ethnicity – another rich source of partial truths, bent truths, and downright dissimulation in anthropology.

The notion of an "ethnic group" has attracted ferocious deconstruction in recent years. Presumably, it is immediately implicated in every attack on the concept of culture, or more particularly of "a" culture (Brightman 1995; Brumann 1999). The current era ought, however, to be more tolerant of ethnology than the one that went before. After all, during the hegemony of high structuralism it was totally thrust aside; indeed, it took on an aura of antiquarian obscurantism. For Claude Lévi-Strauss it hardly mattered how many individuals shared a particular myth or kinship system, or where precisely they lived, since all such myths and systems – collected here, collected there – were only transformations of the underlying structures it was his purpose to reveal (1967: 29–53). In the post-structuralist era, such lofty abstractions are not in vogue, and the details are the essence. Consequently, the tangles and confusions of ethnicity become once again the very stuff of anthropology. Thus encouraged, I continue my narrative.

Lelakness

For most of the nineteenth century, no one lived at the place called Long Teru. All the name then signified was the place where the Teru stream flowed into the main river, a name constructed according to the standard mode of geographical reference in a riverine society. In fact, no one lived anywhere along the banks of the main river because such sites were too vulnerable to attack from war parties sweeping down from the far interior. It was a period of endemic violence, a period of *völkerwanderung*, when old orders were collapsing and whole populations on the move. Those in the far interior, where the rivers ran fast between forest-clad mountains, pressed down towards the coast, displacing others in a chain reaction. One longhouse community, or part of a community, moved here, another there, this one as aggressors, that one as refugees. Smaller communities were liable to annihilation, their members killed or taken off as slaves.

The causes of this chaos seem mainly to concern geopolitics in the outside world. In the nineteenth century, the coastal trading state of Brunei was in decline. At its apogee in the sixteenth century, it commanded tribute from as far away as the southern Philippines and the southwestern corner of Borneo (Brown 1970: 76). Such was its wealth and fame at the time when it was first enountered by Europeans (Pigafetta 1525?) that the whole vast island – bigger than France or Texas – took its name from a corruption of the city's. It was, however, a fragile edifice, prone to the vacillating fortunes that characterized what Stanley Tambiah called the "galactic polities" of southeast Asia (1976: 102–31). The impact of European expansion was to undermine steadily Brunei's control of its sea lanes, and introduce new commodities whose supply Brunei could not match. In Brunei's hinterland, along the rivers that led into the interior, an extensive but slow-moving network of trading links was strained to the point of rupture. New goods stimulated new demands, and ambitious leaders set about gaining wealth by more direct means. Slaves added to the size of their followings, allowing the chaos to be spread yet further afield. The climax came in 1856, when five thousand Kayan raiders, having laid waste the lower reaches of two rivers, camped outside Brunei itself, and a helpless Sultan had to buy them off (St John 1862). Brunei never recovered its confidence, and steadily abandoned its territorial claims.

Meanwhile, small communities in the lower reaches of the main rivers were in even worse danger. They had three choices, if they were not to be wiped out. They could retreat towards the coast, relying on what protection Brunei still had to offer, and in the process being absorbed into coastal Muslim society. Or they could settle their differences with other communities in the lowlands, and come together in villages large enough to defend themselves. Or finally they could retreat into places sufficiently isolated that no one could approach suddenly. The Teru stream offers such a retreat, being narrow, winding, and full of fallen tree trunks. To drag along it one of the massive war canoes used by raiding parties, some able to seat fifty or more paddlers, would be extremely hard work, while any rapid approach by land was thwarted by swamps. There would be plenty of time to flee further into the jungle.

In the 1870s, as colonial records attest, there was a small community living on the banks of a large, shallow lake that could only be reached via the Teru. They called themselves Lelak, and they claimed to have lived near the lake from time immemorial. Unlike almost all peoples in the region, they had no traditions of migration at all – true indigenes. There were no other Lelak communities. Their leader, when first we hear of them, is called Orang Kaya Luwak. Orang Kaya was a title bestowed by the Sultan of Brunei, and its literal meaning, "Rich Man," clearly points to the commercial nature of Brunei's influence. It also points to the place that the Lelak held as middlemen in the ancient trading network of Brunei, which came about because the lower courses of the rivers, flowing through swampy, infertile terrain, had even lower population densities than the far interior. Though few and vulnerable in the late nineteenth century, the Lelak nevertheless had a history not only of independence, but also of relative wealth and sophistication.

Having everything to gain from "pacification," Orang Kaya Luwak early on adopted a policy of cooperation with the Brooke Raj. It was a regime with its own eccentricities, having been founded in the 1840s by an English adventurer, James Brooke, who helped the Sultan suppress a minor rebellion on the southern periphery of Brunei's territory, and was rewarded by being made ruler of a small province, with the subsidiary title of Rajah. Under the energetic leadership first of James and then his successor Charles, the lesser progressively swallowed up the greater. The final acts of that drama, played out in the 1880s, saw control of the whole restless hinterland of Brunei itself ceded to the Raj (Runciman 1960). The biggest slice was the watershed of the Baram river, ceded in 1882 and home to those same Kayan who had terrorized Brunei a generation earlier. Despite their exotic title and personalized rule, however, the Rajahs operated through an administration recognizably in the British colonial pattern, which the first District Officers in Baram set about replicating. Having strictly limited military and financial resources, they could only establish control over the vast area by means of local allies, who, if judiciously chosen, would be only too happy to provide warriors for "punitive expeditions" against old enemies who happened to be recalcitrant to the Raj. The key was to restrain the former from wholesale murder, using only the threat of violence to bring the latter to an accommodation. The resulting *Pax Brookenensis* was celebrated in a series of great formal peacemaking ceremonies that were the most spectacular fruit of the phase of "pacification" (Hose and McDougall 1912: II: 257–310).

In this delicate diplomacy, Orang Kaya Luwak seized every opportunity to play the traditional Lelak role of middleman. He joined the District Officers' expeditions, but he came virtually alone. Instead of warriors, of whom he could muster few, he brought his wits and cunning, and acted as negotiator. As pacification took hold, he found another way to be indispensable. The Lelak position in the old Brunei trading network resulted from the fact that there were no other communities at all in the swampy lower reaches of the Tinjar river. Now the same feature made them invaluable to the District Officer when he visited the once troublesome communities of the upper Tinjar. Going upriver from his little fort at Marudi, he used paddlers recruited locally under a kind of corvée system. However, having ascended a stretch of the Baram river and then the lower reaches of the Tinjar, it was still a long pull all the way to the headwaters. Consequently, it was more reasonable to stop halfway up, take on a new team of paddlers, and let the first go back to Marudi. To facilitate this, sometime before the turn of the century, Orang Kaya Luwak moved the Lelak community away from the lake that had always been their refuge, and down to a new site at the mouth of the Teru stream.

After this move, Long Teru becomes the name not just of a place, but also of a community. It was one that figured on all maps of the era because District Officers going into the Tinjar always stopped there, and since map-making is a conservative business it still does.[1] Moreover, the people of Long Teru began the long familiarity with the English that reached its climax in the person of Penghulu Lawai. All of these distinctions, however, could not mask the fact that Long Teru remained a tiny community compared to some of the huge longhouses found further upriver. Moreover, in the first decades of the twentieth century, it got even smaller. For unknown reasons, birthrates were low, and during my fieldwork in the 1970s old people spoke of a time when the longhouse was unnaturally quiet, seeming to lack life.[2]

Long Teru's shrinking population was revived in the 1920s, not by a renewed Lelak vigor, but by immigration. The immigrants came from a community in the lower reaches of the river Tutoh, another major tributary that branches off from the Baram just above the mouth of the Tinjar. The name of this community has an unusual etymology, but in the interests of telling one story at a time, let me just say that the people of Batu Belah call themselves Melawan. There were, and are, several Melawan longhouses, but in the 1920s the community at Batu Belah was split by bitter factionalism. It was the losing faction at Batu Belah that was invited to come and settle at Long Teru.

Melawan immigrants revived the Lelak community, but at the cost of assimilation. The immigrants and their children intermarried throughout the longhouse, and, lacking any notion of lineal descent, there were no barriers to integration. Meanwhile, the Melawan were culturally aggressive, and within a generation the Lelak language was losing ground. By the time of my fieldwork, it was remembered only by a handful of old people, and in all everyday interactions Melawan had completely replaced it. In terms of the internal politics of the community, it was the immigrants who had allies elsewhere, and it was predominantly their allies and relatives who turned up to longhouse festivals. At the all-important death rituals, the major arena of status competition, it was Melawan who swelled the crowds and made the events a success.

There were just a few contexts in which the Lelak heritage remained supreme, and these all had to do with ritual. Melawan religion, like Lelak, gives emphasis to the ancestors, and at Long Teru the ancestors were unquestionably Lelak. Consequently, in prayers it was the Lelak ancestors who were invoked, sometimes collectively, and sometimes by name, whoever did the praying. Prayers are made in public in a style of language with its own metrical conventions and artistry, and expertise in their delivery is the province of leading men (Metcalf 1989). Consequently, anyone with political ambitions would have to trace some link to leaders of the past, if necessary grafting himself on to the Lelak stock, even as he spoke the prayers in Melawan.

Moreover, there was just one ritual context in which the Lelak language itself survived, and that was in the death songs. In Chapter 2, I pointed out that my tape recordings of the death songs were nearly impossible to transcribe or translate because no one would countenance me playing them when there was no corpse in the longhouse. That problem was compounded by another: some of the key songs were sung in a language for which I possessed barely a word list, let alone a working knowledge. That brings us back to Kasi, who could have translated the Lelak songs for me. I only understood this, however, long after I had settled in with the headman, who was closely associated with the Melawan element. I had always wondered why his apartment was not in the center of the longhouse, which is the normal location for the most elite families. Instead, it was about a third of the way up from the downriver end, the end associated with the Melawan, who arrived from that direction, as did I. Kasi lived a similar distance in from the upriver end, creating a neatly dyadic arrangement. Were I so inclined, I might make a list in the manner of Rodney Needham's famous analysis (1973) of the symbolic powers of the Mugwe of the Meru people of Kenya:

visible to the state	invisible to the state
politics	religion
manifest	esoteric
immigrant	autochthonous
downriver	upriver
mouth	source
male	female

To do it justice, such a structural schema might not only provide an *aide-mémoire* or summary but also hints at some peculiarly Long Teru political dynamics. Nevertheless, we shall need to deal directly with how it was that Kasi came to be the embodiment of Lelakness.

The vanishing point

The most obvious answer is that she was directly descended from the great Lelak leaders of the past. This was an assertion easily elicited, though Kasi herself would never have said it, at least in so many words, since boasting is for a true aristocrat simply not done – a sure sign of the impostor. So it was asserted *about* her, and often with an air of finality as if it settled everything. The problem with this is that same lack of lineal institutions we already noted; in the previous three generations, all the immigrants had acquired Lelak connections, just as all the Lelak had acquired Melawan ones. Just about everybody could claim kinship with the leaders of the past through links matrilateral or patrilateral, affinal or adoptive, or a combination of these, and all such links weighed equally. Moreover, all politically active men, wherever they lived in the longhouse, did just that every time they made a prayer.

Consequently, it is hard to see in Kasi a Lelak version of "the last of the Mohicans." In James Fenimore Cooper's novel, there are no female Mohicans left, and we are given to understand that for that reason the tribe is doomed. Then the old chief Chingachgook loses his only son in warfare, and so becomes the tragic "last." If, however, his son Uncas had lived to marry Cora, and if they had had children, who then would have been "the last"? Cora is portrayed as almost English, the half-sister of the blonde Alice, but nevertheless with a wealthy West Indian Creole connection. The obvious angle for postcolonial criticism is the approach to, and shying away from, the suggestion of miscegenation between a white woman and native man, even though the whiteness of the woman has been carefully qualified. What I notice, however, is the artificiality of making anyone the "last" of anything. Would Uncas, had he not been killed off, have been the last? Or would his children have been Mohicans too, even though they were also part-English and part-African? And what about their children? The issue nowadays cannot be phrased in Cooper's terms. In a world of incessant transnational transfers of genes as well as commodities, how should an ethnicity simply come to a halt?

In this regard, central northern Borneo was always postmodern. Despite its ethnic complexity, or perhaps because of it, intermarriage was no issue, especially as it was the aristocrats who were most inclined to make alliances outside the community. Whatever their ancestry, aristocrats saw themselves as custodians of the community's heritage.[3] Despite the isolation of the Lelak community in the nineteenth century, and its isolationism in the twentieth, still there was a relatively greater tendency for elite families to marry out. As we have seen, Kasi herself had married a prominent man of another community after Lawai's death, rather than settle for a lesser personage from within Long Teru. Moreover, unlike Chingachgook, she had children who had their own families. One of her children with Lawai (the daughter on the right in Figure 10) was adopted from a community neither Lelak nor Melawan, but Iban. The adoption, however, was accomplished through a ritual whose force was to make the child in every jural sense the "descendant" of her parents, so that it became a fineable offense to slander the child's status. By this act, Kasi presumably anointed an Iban inheritor of the Lelak tradition.

What underlay Kasi's special claim to Lelakness was evidently not some notion of unique "ethnic purity." Certainly she possessed advantages of birth, but genealogy alone could not have brought her the standing she held. In the language of a previous generation of political anthropologists, her status was "achieved" rather than "ascribed" (Gluckman 1965), but what did Kasi "achieve"? She had married well, although you could equally say that Lawai had done well to marry her. She had learned some of the death songs, but she told me plainly that when she was a girl everyone knew them. Whenever she sang those songs, she was always surrounded by that group of age-mates, the irreverent old ladies who were her most intimate friends, and I am not sure that they did not know the songs as well as she did. The same might be true for the stories that Kasi told, beginning with her memorable formula, although her friends always claimed that Kasi knew them better, or told them with more flair. In terms of what political anthropologists had in mind, these are insubstantial qualifications.

Nevertheless, Kasi's sense of drama points towards something that might seem even more elusive, but in the end proves more tangible, something similar to what Marilyn Ivy (1995) describes a "discourses of the vanishing". What Ivy is trying to capture with thi phrase is the strange ambivalence that Japanese people manifes towards their own culture. On the one hand, there is constan emphasis on the uniqueness of Japanese ways, so as to project th image of a robust and uniform Japanese culture. On the othe hand, there is an equally constant anxiety that what makes then Japanese is being lost, erased by the twin forces of modernity an Westernization. The result is a veritable fetishization of custom and folkways that are seen to embody an idealized traditiona Japan.

If the whole Japanese nation is concerned about the vanishing c their culture, about things that are in Ivy's phrase "gone but nc quite," then the fate of Lelak culture represents a kind of limitin case, a vanishing point. By the mid-1970s, the Lelak language wa all but gone, and it was hard to point to anything at Long Ter that was unambiguously Lelak, with that one small exception. Iv describes the discourses and practices she recovers as ghostl} "ghosts of stories and (sometimes) stories of ghosts" (1995: 20 and this description fits Kasi's expertise nicely. The stories she tok to her neighbors and grandchildren and me were always about th ancestors, and there was always a certain hazy quality about then I never knew exactly how one story connected to another, or whei mythic heightening began and ended, or what I might grasp at a history or cosmology. The songs she led at the beginning of mortu ary rites took this quality to a higher level; they were opaque to m and hidden, but I knew enough to know that they contained a direc invitation to ancestral shades, a summoning far more specific tha anything contained in prayer.

Given this "ghostliness," was Lelakness a private phantas} given life only by Kasi? An answer is provided by comparing Ka with a religious innovator described by Anna Tsing (1993). Um ("Mother") Adang lived in the sparsely populated mountains i the far southeastern corner of Borneo. It is a region that has bee buffeted by violent historical forces, the struggles of expansionai traditional states and the modernizing efforts of Dutch colonialism and the Indonesian Republic, but always as a half-forgotten margin. Responding to these disruptions in her own way, Uma Adang fashioned for herself a cosmology ruled over by the Diamond Queen, a figure tenuously connected to the Hinduized royal courts of Java and the Islamic sultanate of Banjarmasin. In her rituals, Uma Adang addresses such issues as birth control and evil place spirits, running together "discourses that would have one embrace national, ethnic, or religious identities as badges of commitment to progress and reason – but she stacks together all these discourses, and much more, like items at a rummage sale." Uma Adang's "'postmodern' eclecticism" has the Diamond Queen ruling over a world of "wobbly reproductions" (Tsing 1993: 254, 278).

There are real similarities between the worlds of Uma Adang and Bilo Kasi. The lower Baram area has also known contesting political powers and ideologies, and in the discourses of Upriver People mythic references to the Sultan of Brunei and the White Rajah often jostle with Upriver heroes and anxieties about the modern world. There is a certain eclecticism in the indigenous religions of central northern Borneo, if only because such orthodoxies as exist apply only to single longhouse communities. In moving from one to another, an in-marrying person readily adopts the forms of his or her spouse, mixing them freely with those from home. In prayer, well-traveled men showed off their ability to weave together words and phrases from other languages. Moreover, the new information that may at any time be gained from shamans means that spirit worlds are always open-ended.

Despite these similarities of environment, however, the personal styles of Uma Adang and Kasi could not have been more different. By comparison with the former's prodigal invention, Kasi's narratives seem positively spare, and unlike Uma Adang, she made no obvious attempt to draw attention to herself. Above all she would have scorned the role of innovator; she saw herself strictly as conservator. If, however, Kasi was not guilty of exhibitionism, she remains vulnerable to the charge of snobbery. Her version of

Lelakness gave her a social standing from which she did not hesitate to profit. In Chapter 2, we saw her interfering in other people's affairs, and taking it upon herself to prohibit a ritual in which she had not even been invited to play a part. This was not by any means the only occasion when Kasi might have been described as high-handed, and the fact that she got away with it shows the power of what was, at Long Teru, a hegemonic discourse. Moreover, I might well be accused of subjecting myself to the same hegemony, not only while I lived there and could not avoid it, but in what I write now. I would not be the first writer about central northern Borneo to be seduced by a romance of nobility. Charles Hose, an early District Officer in Baram who wrote extensively about his adventures, was prone to find indigenous aristocrats in the most unlikely places. For instance, in his *Fifty Years of Romance and Research, or, The Diary of a Jungle Wallah*, he describes the noisy Aban Jau, who, in the late nineteenth century, styled himself Rajah of Tinjar, as "this fine old Chief" (Hose 1927: 48). His Melawan followers, by contrast, remember Aban Jau as something of a ruffian, and scoff at his presumption (Metcalf 1992).

To come, then, to the nub of the matter: what should an honest ethnographer report about Lelak ethnicity? By re-presenting Kasi's account of Lelakness, I become her mouthpiece, and make fact out of pretension. But how could I describe Lelakness in the mid-1970s without Kasi? Then again, if I simply describe Long Teru as a Melawan community, and leave out the complications of its Lelak roots, I essentialize the category "Melawan" by tidying it up, and giving it neat edges where none exist. Whichever way I turn, it seems that I am caught in deceptions.

Note also that linguistics provides no easy way out. It is many years since Dell Hymes (1968) warned against any simple identification between language and ethnicity. The crucial intermediate variable, he argues, is the speech community. Since in central Borneo the speech community is the longhouse community, we cannot expect the complexities of the former to resolve the complexities of the latter. Obviously, there is a great deal more to be said about linguistic variability in longhouse communities, but for present purposes we only need note that there would be no sense in partitioning Long Teru between Lelak speakers and Berawan speakers, nor would that help in understanding Kasi's claims to Lelakness.

Here the metaphor of a vanishing point might be pushed further. The term comes of course from those techniques of perspective drawing that Marshall McLuhan saw as key to the emergence of modernism, because they enabled a three-dimensional reality to be precisely inscribed. In his best-known piece of gonzo sociology *The Medium is the Massage* (1969: 52–3), he shows a Renaissance painting of a piazza, paved with slabs of marble edged in black (see Figure 11). The artist's enthusiasm for the new technique of perspective drawing allows no room for subtlety. Relentlessly the black lines converge towards a vanishing point at the horizon, bordered by similarly diminishing buildings and colonnades. As a landscape, it looks to contemporary eyes arid, but at the moment it was painted it must have seemed almost magically graphic, a new insight into the world.

Analogously, the same three-dimensional power attaches to what we might call the ethnographic perspective of modern anthropology, whose impact can only be gauged by comparing it with what went before. In Western folk depictions, the island of Borneo is inhabited by a single, largely unseen, mysterious and uniformly savage population. This flat image provided the perfect painted backdrop for one of the most famous freak acts of the nineteenth century, the Wild Men of Borneo. They were in fact a pair of retarded brothers, Hiram and Barney Davis, who were discovered by an itinerant showman on an Ohio farm in the 1850s. They were muscular dwarves, about three and a half foot tall, with long hair and beards, and sallow complexions. Their act consisted of feats of strength, and the promoter P.T. Barnum dressed them in peculiar striped shirts and leggings, and circulated flyers describing how they had been captured on the coast of Borneo after fierce resistance (Kunhardt *et al.* 1995: 270). This Borneo continues to serve its

Figure 11 Ideal City by Francesco di Georgio Martini; © Staatliche Museen zu Berlin, Preussicher Kulturbesitz, Gemäldegalerie. Photo by Jörg P. Anders, Berlin.

theatrical function. In Domalain's execrable *Panjamon: I Was a Headhunter* (1974), whose publisher's blurb I quoted in Chapter 1, the natives serve as a set of cardboard figures in front of which the author postures. There is, I suppose, a certain amusement to be had from such camp primitivism, but it derives from contemplating the cultural productions of the West, not of Borneo.

By contrast, the perspective provided by modern ethnography reveals a hard-edged reality, Borneo seen in depth. After a century of accumulated effort, it is possible to delineate the numbers and locations of populations, and outline their considerable social, cultural, and linguistic diversity. Whatever the faults of Borneo ethnography, this is a substantial achievement. Given the relatively small amount of professional fieldwork that has been conducted in Borneo, much of the credit goes to untrained amateurs. Some were colonial administrators, others were local people who took an interest in their own cultures, but all of them resisted the temptation to sensationalize and tried instead to render plainly what they observed. Their work furnishes an extraordinary and invaluable archive.

The ethnographic perspective works best, however, with straight lines, or at least definite shapes. In ethnographic terms, that means finding just those neat edges that I could not put around the Lelak. For colonial officers, it was an administrative reflex to set about sorting out and labeling the various ethnic groups and subgroups. The first anthropologists on the scene readily continued the same project. When this turned out more difficult than expected, the quest became an obsession, a holy grail, obscuring everything else. In my preparation for fieldwork, I pored over standard works on Borneo, and discovered a peculiar thing: they all contained different lists of ethnic group names. So, for instance, the guide produced by the Human Relations Area File to the *Ethnic Groups of Insular Southeast Asia* (Lebar 1972) provides eleven main categories for the peoples of Borneo, while the *Bibliography of Indonesian Peoples and Cultures* (Kennedy 1974) sorts them under eight categories. The two lists have just one category in common – not much progress for a century of ethnology.

If the example of the virtually extinct Lelak is too slight to convince the reader of the problems of ethnic classification in central Borneo, let me provide a few others.

Foregrounding the Berawan

A commonsense response to my dilemmas about dealing with Lelak ethnicity might be to ask why, if I had wanted to work with the Melawan, I didn't just choose a Melawan village in the first place. It would be an appropriate question, since there are classic cases of anthropologists claiming to say something generally about a population based on studies in markedly untypical places, or even among people not in the supposed population at all. For instance, Francis Hsu's study subtitled *Chinese Culture and Personality* (1948) was based on research in a village in Yunnan – hardly the heartland of Chinese culture – and among an ethnic minority called Bai, who had their own kingdom independent of the Chinese Emperors, and who speak a language that may not be in the Sinitic family at all. Hsu's case is egregious, but it does not follow that the truth can be delivered by some process of statistical sampling, either in China or in Borneo. To draw a sample, the statistician must first bound a population, and it is precisely at this stage that we come undone. If we sidestepped Kasi, from among whom at Long Teru should we select the typical Lelak?

If the Lelak situation is hopelessly confused, however, can I do better in specifying the Melawan population? It might be taken as a bad sign that, even before I begin, I am having trouble choosing the right name. In Chapter 1 I spoke of doing fieldwork among the Berawan, whereas I referred to the immigrants who arrived at Long Teru in the 1920s as Melawan. What could possibly be the problem here? The answer, as usual, is not so simple. Generally speaking, ethnographers have come to rely on autonyms – names people use for themselves – because we can be at least moderately confident that they reflect a locally salient category. By contrast, Borneo ethnology is littered with terms made up by outsiders that reflect no social reality at all. For instance, Charles Hose, the self-styled jungle wallah, was sharp enough to notice that there were several small ethnic groups in the Baram that really did not fit into any of the major ethnic cohesions. His solution was to lump them all together in a rag-bag category, which he grandly called Klemantan. There are, however, no people who call themselves Klemantan, and the various communities have no sense of being related. As an ethnological category it is also useless, since the people lumped together show no evidence of any common relationship, linguistic or otherwise. Nevertheless, by mere repetition, and quite aside from anything happening in Borneo, the word took on an existence of its own sufficient to gain it a place on the list of major ethnic categories in Kennedy's *Bibliography* (1974).

In the earnest pursuit of autonyms, the first problem is usually that they are not used at all. When people in the longhouses I knew referred to themselves, they usually spoke of *dé kita*, the very pronouns that occur in Kasi's formula for beginning a story. The best gloss would be something like "us lot," and it has a wonderfully elastic referent by no means restricted to ethnicity. They may, however, in speaking to each other in Melawan, refer to themselves as Melawan, so it appears that this is a true autonym. But Melawan people do not only speak Melawan. In their interactions with a wide range of people from the coast or from other longhouse communities, they often speak a variety of Malay that is the lingua franca of the Baram watershed. Now it so happens that the word *melawan* contains an absurd little pun. The Malay root *lawan* means an enemy, and an inflected form with the verbal prefix *me-* sounds almost like a challenge. This is additionally embarrassing because the Melawan had a great reputation in the nineteenth century as berserkers. To avoid these unwanted connotations, when speaking to outsiders Melawan people vary the autonym slightly, and call themselves Berawan. Both Melawan and Berawan are autonyms in a way, but it is the latter that is known thoughout the Baram, and indeed beyond, since the name has made its way into print. For instance, from the writings of Spenser St John (1862) something of the Berawan was known to Edward Burnett Tylor (1964 [1878]: 5), who passed the information on to his student James Frazer. So it is that the Berawan appear in *The Golden Bough*, even in the abridged edition (1922: 17), which is more than you can say for the Nuer, the Trobrianders, or the Tikopia. This is a powerful precedent, but I was not influenced by it when I arrived at Long Teru. The point is that I was given the name Berawan, even by Melawan speakers, because I was an outsider, and once again I am trapped in half-truths.

Once a search for autonyms has been started, however, the next problem is that there are too many of them. The immigrants to Long Teru came from a place called Batu Belah, which looks like a perfectly plausible Malay name meaning something like "Split Rocks," but it is nothing of the sort. If you asked to see the split rocks in question, you would be told that they were miles away in the mountains, in a turbulent tributary of the Baram called the Akah, and, moreover, that properly speaking they were red rocks. Making any sense of this requires what all Berawan communities can provide richly, and only truly indigenous communities like the the Lelak managed to do without, namely migration narratives. The people of Batu Belah tell of ancestors moving out of their mountain fastnesses long before the chaos of the nineteenth century, and descending the Baram in leisurely fashion. At one point, they settled in the headwaters of the Akah, where a red pigment could be obtained. This they used liberally to decorate their shields, and so became the Bitokala, *bito'* meaning stone and *kala* red. Batu Belah is merely an alliterative approximation in Malay manufactured in the nineteenth century by traders from Brunei.

A feature demonstrated by the case of Batu Belah is the irresolvable ambiguity between place names and ethnic names. The true autonym, or perhaps it would be better to say the interior autonym, is Bitokala. In speaking to outsiders in Malay, however, the place name Batu Belah, which is anyway only a pseudo-place name, gets used in exactly the same contexts as Bitokala is used when speaking to other Bitokala. The contrast is no different to the Melawan/ Berawan pair, except that the Malayized version appears to have a geographical referent, and is shown on maps as if it did, and consequently it now does. This complicates matters enormously, because an endless list of place names can now potentially be added to an already bulging list of variously derived autonyms, and this is exactly what has happened in Borneo ethnology. Moreover, the phenomenon is not unique to Borneo, and shows how fruitless it will be to search for any absolute criterion that will finally segregate any list of pure ethnonyms anywhere (Barth 1969; Eriksen 1993; Hutchinson and Smith 1996).

As a further complication, the elite Bitokala families claim a second cultural heritage as well, that of the Pelutan, as a result of intermarriage. In other places perhaps, the Pelutan title might be represented as the name of a clan, rather than that of an ethnic group, but the absence of any notion of descent groups makes this distinction untenable. Nor is it much help to mobilize the term "house" that Lévi-Strauss coined in his later writing on kinship (Carsten and Hugh-Jones 1995), because it collapses immediately into the "longhouse" community, which must be the point of articulation with whatever we are going to call ethnicity in the lower Baram region. The best account of Pelutanness is that it resembles Lelakness at Long Teru, but at a more advanced stage. According to Bitokala migration stories, the Pelutan were a small autochthonous community that they encountered soon after they moved into the lowlands, probably in the eighteenth century. By the 1970s, there was nothing left of the Pelutan language and nothing that anyone could point to that was Pelutan rather than Berawan. All that was left was the name itself, and in contrast to Long Teru it did not stand in terminological opposition to Berawan, but had been assimilated into the very core of Bitokalaness; the most elite Bitokala were Pelutan.

The Pelutan were not the only people the Bitokala met in the lower Baram. In the nineteenth century they shared a massive, fortified longhouse with the people who now live at a place called Long Kiput, not far from Batu Belah. Long Kiput looks as if it should be the place where the Kiput river joins the main Baram, but there is no Kiput river. Once again we are dealing with a *faux* place name, manufactured to look transparent both to Malay traders and to unrelated longhouse-dwelling peoples, a corruption of the true autonym: Lakipo. There was no possibility, however, that the Berawan would assimilate the numerous Lakipo, and despite a close historical association and many cultural similarities, the Lakipo do not choose to identify themselves as Berawan (or Melawan).

There is a third longhouse not far from Batu Belah where people do claim Berawan identity. However, at Long Terawan the most frequently offered autonym is Long Pata, that being a place in the mountains where their ancestors were settled for a long time and had glorious martial episodes. When the Long Pata people finally moved into the lowlands towards the end of the nineteenth century they absorbed a remnant of the Tring people, who had once been very numerous but had suffered badly in the warfare of that time. Consequently, the Tring occupy something of the same status at Long Terawan that the Lelak do at Long Teru, except that they have always been treated as clients by the leading families of the Long Pata, who maintained marriage alliances with powerful communities upriver. Nevertheless, the combination of Tring and Berawan makes one wonder about the name Terawan. This time there really is a Terawan river, but by now we have learned to look sideways at all such names. Is it possible that the river was named after the community, rather than the reverse, a deceit masked by the prefix "long"?

At this point, the reader might reasonably throw up his or her hands and say: enough! In the last few paragraphs, proper nouns have accumulated rapidly, and the details soon become laborious. Edie Turner recalls that Meyer Fortes used to drive everybody insane by constantly modifying every statement he made about the Talle with exceptions, caveats, and disclaimers (Engelke 1998: 28).

Evidently he had to deal with a situation not dissimiliar to central northern Borneo, and it is noticeable that he speaks of a "congeries" (*Oxford English Dictionary*: "mass, heap") of tribes in the northern part of Ghana (Fortes 1940: 239). Fortes was evidently concerned about just those issues that now prompt a critique of the notion of "an ethnic group," but his response to them was apparently a conversation stopper.

Moreover, since Clifford Geertz (1988) taught us to pay attention to the style of anthropological writing as well as its content, the piling up of mere data must be suspect, tempting a reading that examines "what is excluded, what is concealed" (Rosenau 1992: 120). But I have already deconstructed the obsessive collection of ethnic group names in the literature on Borneo, and I am aware only of trying to restrain the details from getting even further out of hand. What I offer here is the barest possible outline distilled from innumerable tangled conversations held over many months. That does not imply, however, that in those conversations anyone was trying to conceal anything from me. On the contrary, they were trying to feed me the information that they thought I could digest. It would be perverse to complain that my "data" were "rich."

Lost tribes

Given this superfluity of names, it is not hard to discover "lost tribes." The most famous case in this genre in recent years was the Tasaday, a supposedly stone-age people discovered living in a cave in a remote corner of the Philippines in the early 1970s. After the first sensational announcements and articles in the *National Geographic*, it was not long before there were accusations that the discovery was a hoax. One might have thought that one long sober look by an anthropologist would have settled the question, and it did no good to the reputation of the discipline when it appeared that there were professionals who grew heated on both sides of the controversy. In an attempt to restore order in the ranks, the American Anthropology Association sponsored a special session on the topic at its annual meetings in 1988, bringing together many of those who had visited the Tasaday. No consensus resulted, as can be seen in the resulting volume *The Tasaday Controversy: Assessing the Evidence* (1992) edited by Thomas Headland.

Two supporters of the early reports, Amelia Rogel-Rara and Emmanuel Nabayra (1992), take aim at the problem with that familiar anthropological blunderbuss, the genealogical method. They sort the cave population into three classes: "26 full-blooded 'Real Tasaday'," "22 half-blooded Tasaday," and "22 persons with no Tasaday blood but considered by the community as 'Tasaday' by marriage or adoption and residence." In this list there is a strange mixture of criteria. Do the Tasaday themselves consider that in-marrying spouses are "Tasaday" rather than Tasaday, and how is that expressed? What about the "half-blooded"? Are they Tasaday or "Tasaday" or is there an expression for "half-Tasaday"? Presumably the point of all this is that there was once a population that was all "real Tasaday," but strangely enough "the earliest progenitors (G-0) recalled by the elder Tasaday were Lubas (male), who lived in Tasaday, and Layas (female), who came from the Tasafang, one of two interior groups with whom the Tasaday socially interacted in the past" (Rogel-Rara and Nabayra 1992: 91, 94). Doesn't that make the children of Lubas and Layas "half-blooded," and weren't they ancestors to the "26 full-blooded" Tasaday?

The subtitle of the book asserts a positivist premise: that there is "evidence" that, when "assessed," will settle the controversies. Against that premise stands the continuing lack of consensus, which might result from some mix of deceit, gullibility, obstinacy, or error, but might just as easily indicate that the contestants are talking at cross-purposes. In the first lines of both his Preface and his Introduction, Headland speaks of "the people called Tasaday," but he does not tell us who calls them that. In his Introduction, he lists nineteen "Immediate Scientific Questions," covering such things as use of stone tools, cave dwelling, and foraging, but he raises no question about the name itself. Rogel-Rara and Nabayra speak of Lubas living "in" Tasaday, so is it a place name? If that turned out to be so, would a "half-Tasaday" be a commuter? Are there no Tasaday who married out of the stone age, which seems on the face of it a more attractive option than moving in? Is there a particle *tasa*, as in Tasaday and Tasafeng, and if so, what does it mean? If Tasaday is asserted to be an autonym, in what circumstances was it first recorded? If the Tasaday were as cut off from other people as some would have us believe, what made it worthwhile having an autonym at all? How can we be sure that the name wasn't made up by someone else, and imposed?

The one thing that no one disputes about the Tasaday is that they are called the Tasaday. The same applies to the Pelutan, and since their name has never before appeared in print, they also constitute a lost tribe, now, thankfully, discovered to science. It might be argued that those people at Batu Belah who call themselves Pelutan cannot be lost because even the government knew they were there; they have been interviewed for the Malaysian census. But the lesser efficiency of the Philippine government is surely neither here nor there for the ethnologist; it is their Pelutanness that was "lost." Again, it might be objected that those people are not Pelutan because they are really Bitokala. But the Bitokala are also Berawan (and Melawan), and being the latter in no way excludes being the former.

The true Berawan

I have described Berawan communities at Long Teru, Batu Belah, and Long Terawan. Those most inclined to assert their Berawan identity, however, are the people who now live at Long Jegan, in the middle reaches of the river Tinjar. In fact, they call themselves *Melawan tu'o*, the "true Berawan," reflecting a certain distance from other Berawan. What gave them that distance was a different migration route from the mountains, not via the Baram river but down the Tinjar, and for a long historical period they evidently had the entire watershed to themselves, apart from the Lelak in the far lower reaches. This gives them a sense of isolation and continuity. Not surprisingly, however, other Berawan are not inclined to concede any superior authenticity. Instead, they point to the period during the stormy late nineteenth century when the ancestors of the Long Jegan people found it advantageous to ally themselves in a single longhouse community with an aggressive new wave of immigrants in the Tinjar, under the leadership of that "fine old Chief" and upstart bully Aban Jau. Who exactly those immigrants were I shall not tell just now – I must stop somewhere – suffice it to say that unlike all the peoples so far mentioned, Lelak, Berawan, Tring, Lakipo, they did not practice secondary treatment of the dead. In particular, they shunned the practice – common to all the others mentioned above – of opening coffins months or years after the first storage, cleaning the bones, and storing them finally in a new location. In sharing a community with these secondary-treatment-shunning newcomers, the ancestors of the Long Jegan people adopted various ritual compromises that, according to other Berawan, make them virtually apostate – so much for the "true Berawan."

Meanwhile, the Berawan of Batu Belah and Long Teru, first cousins after all, sometimes refer to themselves as *Melawan tenga'* or "middle Berawan" with all the expansiveness of the Han Chinese referring to themselves as the Middle Kingdom. There is indeed in these stories an uncanny echo of world history, so that it is easy, sitting round a wick lantern and listening to the sagas, to imagine that one is hearing about centuries rather than decades, and empires and nations rather than tribelets and longhouses. If the details of my narrative are confusing, would it be easier to explain what populations made up the Carolingian empire, or why its capital cities were moved from here to there, or how it relates to the Capetian dynasty that followed, and how the Angevins fit in to all that? Why should the history of the various nations of the Berawan and their sometime allies, though on a smaller scale, be any less complex than the history of Europe? In both contexts, an ethnographic perspective gives a similar view of broad categories directly in front of the viewer, a more busy middle ground with all kinds of distracting scenery in view, all seeming to diminish into one point – Europe, Borneo – in the far distance.

To move the point of vantage changes the view certainly, but not the nature of the perspective. In the 1970s, the longhouse at Long Jegan was a splendid old structure that contained timbers taken from the longhouse where Aban Jau had held sway. It was built, however, in three sections, connected by little bridges. These sections memorialized the fact that the Berawan followers of Aban Jau had not always been united. After the collapse of Aban Jau's community, old factions reemerged, and went their different ways. It was some time before they were reunited by a new leader whose genius it was to pull the dispersed elements together. Decades later, however, sitting in any one part of the trifurcated longhouse, people who had been cohabiting and intermarrying for generations would warn me against the dubious character of those Other people – their neighbors across the little bridges.

This example makes plain the paradox of ethnicity: nothing ever exists in pure form, and nothing ever goes away.

The quality of world-in-miniature suggests a continuity of issues between longhouse and nation. Richard Handler's study of Québecois nationalism focuses on "the naturalizing and objectifying presuppositions that sustain the undeniable existence of a Québecois nation" (1988: 18). Handler adopts this strategy because he is suspicious of historical accounts of French Canada. By narrating the Québecois nation, he argues, social scientists trap themselves into presenting a real and unquestionable entity, and so lose all power of observing how it is constructed. In this way they become a part of the process of "cultural objectification" rather than observers of the process. He pays attention instead to contexts where national culture is self-consciously celebrated, such as folk dance performances and museums of *patrimoine*. In the rhetorics of "ethnic mobilization" he finds metaphors of the nation as living being, and the British conquest as rape (1988: 14–15). There is in

Handler's strategy a certain element of exposé, not so much of deception as manipulation, of what's going on behind the scenes of nationalist activism.

Can this cultural critique be extended to ethnography in interior Borneo? Handler's concern is specifically with modern nationalist ideologies founded on Western notions of individualism (1988: 50–1). Nevertheless, there may be parallels in a politics of culture that is played out within longhouse communities. For instance, the leader, Tama Lire, who pulled together the Long Jegan community after its generation-long diaspora certainly achieved some kind of "ethnic mobilization," and it would be fascinating to know in what terms that was phrased. In the previous epoch, longhouse communities large enough to defend themselves were a neccessity of survival, and figures like Aban Jau emerged along with them. Tama Lire, however, had no such goad; under the *Pax Brookenensis* and with almost unlimited supplies of land it is hard to see any material advantage in centralized living sites. It follows that Tama Lire appealed to the values of community *per se*, some mixture of aristocratic hauteur and social density, of the sheer rightness and grandeur of the longhouse. Sometimes in the 1970s I fancied I could hear the echo of his rhetoric in the way that people at Long Jegan talked about their metropolis as if it were the center of the civilized world, their Paris, their Rome.

As for processes of "cultural objectification," they also must be located outside of modernist ideologies, and the crucial arena is ritual. The longhouse is, perhaps before anything else, a ritual community, a "congregation" in the fullest Durkheimian sense. The power of this understanding of community is demonstrated by the elaborate ritual compromises reached by the followers of Aban Jau. We have already noticed that the self-styled "true Berawan" were driven to drop certain mortuary practices involving moving corpses about and cleaning their bones, but their co-residents also made modifications, developing in effect phenomenally long funerals. One party claimed to be practicing secondary treatment of the dead while the other denied that they were, but what mattered was the appearance of common practice, common enough at least that each side could participate in the funerals of the other. It was an uncomfortable compromise, but essential, because there could be no community without universal participation in major long-house festivals. Moreover, each party retained the ritual compromises after the alliance was dissolved. Ritual, in short, manifests that same quality of neither existing in pure forms, nor ever going away, that we noted as characteristic of ethnicity, or perhaps indeed it constitutes that quality in Borneo.

There is, however, a reverse side to the ritual consensus of the longhouse. On any particular occasion, all manner of contingent circumstances may be taken into account in designing a rite. If, for instance, a man married into a longhouse, the practices of his home community will be taken into account at his funeral. What ensues is a long and sometimes heated debate on exactly the right way to do things, in which everyone has a say – the surviving spouse, the elders of the family, the visiting in-laws, the leading families, even the dead man if he left specific requests, though he is as likely to be ignored as anyone else. These are the forums in which "cultural objectification" can be seen at work. Ritual provides the content of ethnicity, but in the process it does not essentialize ethnicity. It does not necessarily privilege one over another, Berawan over Bitokala, say, or Bitokala over Pelutan; all can be included. Nor does it exclude other personal life experiences, such as shamans' prescriptions and dream inspirations. In longhouse society, ritual provides an equivalent of Lévi-Strauss' famous "totemic operator," which, by a process of assembling and dismantling elements, could produce the social group at one end and the individual at the other (Lévi-Strauss 1967: 156).

As a cultural critic, my job is to show the workings of this process. The next question is to what extent in doing so I become myself an agent of "cultural objectification," beyond what occurs in the longhouse. In contrast to Handler, I do not have the luxury of taking history for granted as a background, pretty much familiar to everyone who is likely to read what I write, or at worst available in standard histories. On the contrary, I must be the historical narrator as well, and so become a manufacturer of *patrimoine*, especially as I was charged to "make the Berawan name big."

Keeping things in perspective

In the subtitles of two books, *Berawan Eschatology from Its Rituals* (1982) and *Style and Theme in Berawan Prayer* (1989), I have seized on one particular ethnicity as my object. There is an element of shorthand in this; I could hardly put on the title page all the caveats and reservations noted above. Even Meyer Fortes did not do that. Moreover, it is the eschatology and prayer of the Berawan that the books are about, rather than anybody else's. Nevertheless, the use of an ethnonym implicates me, however minimally, in the type of classification that I have just deconstructed. The question we must then ask is: exactly what distortions are involved in that? Certainly there are people who call themselves Berawan, and there are contexts in which their Berawanness matters to them; it is unmistakably a social fact. But what beyond that? Are there in fact specifically Berawan things, such as eschatology or prayer?

In order to answer the question as directly as possible, let me take the example of mortuary practices, which have the advantage that their allowable permutations and combinations are the object of explicit discussion. Every longhouse has features that are character-istic of, and unique to, that community. This is one aspect of the ritual consensus by virtue of which communities function as a congregation. There is, however, no feature that is characteristic of, and unique to, all the Berawan longhouses as contrasted to all non-Berawan longhouses. Putting it another way, there is no ritual consensus associated with Berawanness. So, for instance, the death rites of Batu Belah more closely resemble those of Long Kiput than they do those of Long Jegan, even though the latter is a Berawan longhouse and the former is not. For once, I can even explain why that is the case. As described above, it has to do with events in the late nineteenth century, when some Berawan for reasons of defense shared a community with newly arrived immigrants whose mortuary rituals were radically different to their own. Meanwhile, the remaining Berawan chose allies whose practices were such as to require only minor – though distinctive – changes. Perhaps my 1982 book should be entitled, in nineteenth-century fashion: "Remarks on the Mortuary Rituals of the Berawan of Batu Belah, Long Teru and Long Terawan, together with those of the Lelak, Pelutan, Tring and Lakipo, with a Note on the Berawan of Long Jegan."

Strictly speaking, there are no specifically Berawan death rites. To the extent that I imply that there are, I am involved in reification. What I can show is ritual variation, but that variation is only indirectly correlated with ethnicity, it is not coterminous with it. This is the distortion produced by the ethnographic perspective in the present case. In regard to other matters, or in other places, the specifics may be different, and, as we have seen, there are worse untruths. Nevertheless, in identifying cultural difference – Berawan vs the rest – anthropologists are inescapably caught up in distortions. They illustrate what Roy Wagner meant by "the invention of culture" (1975). This has two aspects, both, in Gregory Bateson's terms, schismogenic (1958). The first proceeds within and between groups, in the case of longhouse society as the "ritual operator" simultaneously constructs individuals and communities. In the second, by describing this process "we turn its indigenous creativity into something arbitrary and questionable, a mere symbolic word play. It becomes 'another Culture,' an analogue of our collective, rationally conceived enterprise" (Wagner 1975: 144). There is in this an echo of Spivak's complaint that anthropology is caught up in "imperialist subject-constitution" (1994: 90).

The deceptive quality of perspective has in fact always been in evidence. The latest edition of the venerable *Brewer's Dictionary of Phrase and Fable* offers this definition:

Trompe l'œil (French, "deception of the eye"). A trick of the eye; a visual deception. It is applied to art that gives a distinct impres-

sion of reality, as, for example, perspective art, which can give a
sense of distance, solidarity and space. The apparent dimensions
of an interior can be magnified by such decorative effects.

(Room 1999: 1203)

Ethnography may be taken as just such an "interior," from which
we have the illusion of looking out onto broader prospects. Its
"magnifying" effect depends on the practitioner controlling the
observer's point of view, because the deception cannot be maintained from several points of view simultaneously. Occasionally,
we even have that *frisson* of disorientation that we associate with
trompe l'oeil when the illusion is suddenly lost, as for instance in
Jim Clifford's (1986) revelations of "ethnographic allegories," of
which the ethnographic perspective is perhaps the most ubiquitous
and least obvious.

In more familiar contexts, however, the graphic effects of perspective are utilitarian and offer no such *frisson*. An architectural
draughtsman does not expect his drawings to be seen as anything
other than sheets of paper on a table; the trick is for him to show
first one view and then another, so allowing those familiar with
their conventions to form a mental image of a structure. The
power of the technique is vastly increased by computer applications
that permit the generation of an unlimited number of views, but its
conventions remain the same.

The anthropological analogue of a draughtman's perspective is
what we have come to call a "situated" discourse – one providing
a perspective – and it has been attributed similar virtues. Stuart
Hall, for instance, argues that any monolithic conception of
"black" identity is subverted by taking account of the way that the
work of Afro-Caribbean writers and film makers is socially and
historically "positioned." Although ethnic histories have their own
reality and are "not mere tricks of the imagination," they tend to fix
identities in a "straight, unbroken line, from some fixed origin"
(1996: 113). In contrast, he emphasizes a dialogic process, creating
difference as well as similarity. What he wants is a multiplicity of

views. Similarly, Donna Haraway argues for situated knowledges both for feminist perspectives and for different positions within feminism. Her anxiety is with the "curious and inescapable term 'objectivity'," and she wonders whether it can be dispensed with or rehabilitated. "'Our' problem," she says, "is how to have *simultaneously* an account of radical historical contingency for all knowledge claims" and "a no-nonsense commitment to faithful accounts of a 'real' world" (1991: 187, italics in original). The latter she sees as necessary to any kind of political activism. Her solution is a "commitment to mobile positioning and to passionate detachment" (1991: 192).

What I have called the ethnographic perspective is, at its best, an example of mobile positioning. What the ethnographer can do, in a way that it is very hard for any particular informant to do, is shift the point of vantage repeatedly, placing first this ethnicity in the foreground, and then another, within some fairly restricted field. None of this is to deny the subject positioning of the ethnographer, nor to disclaim that "objectification" is the result, as much as "objectivity." It is simply the best that can be done. The world is not paved with ethnic groups, but the alternative is not to refuse to see cultural variation, like the "see no evil" monkey. In the nineteenth century, the standard tactic of explorers was to lump together all the peoples of interior Borneo, and to generalize broadly about the "Dayaks." For the ethnographer of Borneo, such a flattening of cultural difference, such a blind suppression of the jumbled, knotty, unfolding complexity of Upriver life, would be the greatest lie of all.

5 Closure

Why did Kasi obstruct my research? I never discussed it with her because both of us were playing a shadow game. In her last years she remained formidable, but as her health declined she also became difficult, even for her family. I am left with a loose end, part of the wistful sense of unfinished business that seems inherent in fieldwork. I feel more sympathy with Kasi's motives now, not because she explained them to me, but because of what has happened in the interim. I am no longer the insecure graduate student. I have published some things, including the monograph whose existence she chooses to acknowledge in her own peculiar way. More importantly, everything has changed in central northern Borneo. Kasi foresaw a future that would sweep away everything that had made her life meaningful, and events have far exceeded her worst fears. I can now appreciate her obstruction as part of a quiet resistance to social forces she very well knew she could not control.

"Lelak"

Kasi's *amour-propre* was bound up with Lelak ancestry and noble lineage. Viewed as an ethnicity, Lelakness approaches a vanishing point, but as a claim to personal status it had far more content than Pelutanness had at Batu Belah. Among the leading families of the Bitokala, the faint echo of remote autochthons gave little more than éclat, rather like the enchantress progenitor of the Plantagenets, who supposedly endowed them with brilliant but mercurial tempers (Kelly 1971: 170). Kasi by contrast engaged in an elaborate self-narration, backed up in crucial ritual contexts, and by the frequently invoked power of ancestors both named and anonymous.

This creative quality is what I mean to indicate by Lelakness, in much the same way as John Pemberton (1994) writes of a "Java" bracketed by inverted commas. The Java he reveals is not a geographical space, but a conception of the authentically Javanese, whose vagaries in the nineteenth and twentieth centuries he fascinatingly traces. The central characters of his story – I am tempted to say its heroes – are the dynasty of superannuated rulers in Surakarta who took the name Pakubuwana, from II to XII. As their direct political influence declined in the face of steadily tightening Dutch colonial control, they responded by creating a sort of inner world that became iconic both for the Javanese and for the Dutch. They created a "Java style" in such things as court costume that melded elements of East and West – formal black jacket worn over batik sarong – but nevertheless became instantly "authentic" (1994: 110–12). On every hand, they elaborated court rituals, mixing in equal parts grand pretensions, mystical references, and personal eccentricities.

Pemberton is careful not to overstate the element of resistance in this. It is hard to argue that these puppet rulers much impeded the Dutch from their exploitative policies. In fact, it would be easier to argue that they were collaborators, preserving their own privileges by becoming pensionaries of the Dutch. The best that can be said is that they turned the fictions of indirect rule back against the Dutch, obliging the masters to play games their clients invented, and to worry about possible snubs in an ever more complex regime of etiquette (Pemberton 1994: 68–70). They led the Dutch a merry dance, and in the process created a cultural space for themselves, which has had significance well into the postcolonial era. Under

Suharto, the struggle continued to control the charismatic resources of the court.

Though the comparison might shock Javanologists, there are parallels with Kasi's chosen role. She also was implicated in a colonial order, through her husband Lawai, and she managed to create a space in which District Officers on the longhouse equivalent of state visits were obliged to comply with local custom as she defined it, draining their glasses when instructed, and dancing ineptly for the general amusement. At the same time, her prestige within the colonial system helped to establish her as a cultural arbiter in her own community. Later, she was suspicious of an "independence" whose rhetoric she presciently did not trust. What is less easy to see in Kasi's case, however, is the creative aspect, largely because I have no record of Lelakness other than hers.[1] In the opening formula of her narrations of Lelak myth and history, she points to what "they" said, framing what "we" say as simple repetition, even if "lies." Other than to admire her artistry of telling, I cannot gainsay her. As for the death songs, there does not seem to be much room for syncretism there, since she could sing them only with the help of her friends, nor is there anything obvious to be gained from innovating.

Consequently, I am forced to collapse two ethnological functions. Pemberton describes how Dutch scholars of Java were rapidly seduced into substituting the "Java" of the courts, especially as the latter produced piles of written texts. In the Javanological study groups set up in the 1920s and 1930s, aristocrats mixed with Europeans. One royal prince in particular gave talks at the palace in Dutch designed to define *de echt-Javaansche national geest*, "the genuine Javanese national spirit" (Pemberton 1994: 129–30). In this way the dual processes of cultural "invention," in Roy Wagner's terms, went on simultaneously, self-discovery immediately followed by inscription. In regard to Kasi's narratives, I am in something of the same position: I consumed them as meekly as the colonial officers before me drank up their rice wine. I may comfort myself that Kasi did not need my help to establish her ideological hegemony at Long Teru, but what part I play in extending it now, as opposed to deconstructing it, is less clear.

Despite these deceptions, if that's what they were, the impression that Pemberton leaves is one of struggle against long odds. The remaining significance of the Javanese courts, eroded by the Dutch, was soon put to the test in a bitter anticolonial war, followed by two very different but self-consciously modernizing regimes. One thing they did not have to cope with, however, as did Kasi's little realm, was wholesale conversion to Christianity.

Throwing out the old way

By the mid-1970s, Long Teru was an island of conservatism in a sea of conversion. In the Baram watershed, the process began just after the Second World War with a series of mass conversions of whole longhouse communities near the headwaters. At one point in 1946, two missionaries – one Anglo-Catholic, the other from the Australian fundamentalist Borneo Evangelical Mission – were leap-frogging along the upper Baram, making converts as fast as they could go and creating a religious division that persists to this day. At the time it was said "the Baram flows backwards" because the new faith reversed the centuries-old direction of acculturation, starting in the far interior and moving downriver. Given all this effervescence, it is strange that the process of conversion was and is characterized in negative terms; it is invariably described with the Malay phrase *buang adat lama*, "throwing out the old way."

In the 1950s the pace of conversion slowed, and there was a counter-stroke, in the form of an indigenous revival focusing on the female deity Bungan. The followers of Bungan copied the organization of the missions, sending apostles from one longhouse to the next to convert people, and even trying to write their own bible. Their principal appeal was simplification; in place of the endless complexities of the old rites, different in every community, they substituted uniform and radically abbreviated rites. Longhouse festivals were abolished wholesale, along with the inconvenient observances associated with the omen birds. Adherents saw the Bungan as a modernizing force, and there was much talk of the time and money saved, a sort of ritual efficiency. The real effect of the Bungan, however, was to undermine the power of the ancestors, and in this way it only served to prepare the way for Christianity. In the mid-1960s, Bungan was gaining as many converts as Christianity, and even recovering converts from Christianity, but by the mid-1970s, it was losing ground everywhere in Baram.[2]

In all this religious turmoil, the Berawan longhouses each went their own way, but there was intense debate within communities to try to preserve unity. All four hung back for a long time, being relatively isolated from Upriver influences. Moreover, their involvement in the Bungan cult was inhibited by the lack of any such female deity in their cosmology, in contrast to most Upriver religions. Slowly, however, the old ways were compromised. At Long Terawan, Protestant influence was strong because the people there were in touch with Kelabit houses in the upper Tutoh that had been early converts of the Borneo Evangelical Mission. The leading families, however, drawn by their alliances to the Kenyah elite in the upper Baram, preferred Catholicism. At Batu Belah there was experimentation with Bungan, but it did not take hold, and eventually the majority decided to back Catholicism. It was at Long Jegan, however, among the "true Berawan," that debate was most intense. Everyone agreed that religion should not be allowed to split the house, but beyond that all was discord. Catholic influence was strong because of the presence of a mission station not far upriver, complete with school and clinic. One party dreaded the abandonment of the ancestors. Another preferred Catholicism but would not have Bungan, arguing that it was just as alien as Christianity, but without the advantages. A third party was prepared to accept Bungan, but would not have Christianity, which it saw as too radical a break with the ancestors. Just to complete all the logical possibilities, a fourth faction seized on the notion that the old death rituals were bringing infertility to the community, and wanted either Bungan or Christianity as long as the old rites were abandoned. Eventually, the situation was saved by the emergence of an indigenous Berawan prophet, Sadi Pejong, who was inspired to reinvent Bungan specifically for a Berawan audience, and so drew almost everyone into a synthesis that lasted through his lifetime (Metcalf 1989: 214–56).

Meanwhile, Long Teru, alone of all the longhouses in the Baram region, rejected apostasy of any kind. Throughout the turmoil of the 1960s, a solid majority persisted in their old and distinctive rites, and their conservatism seemed to be made up of equal parts of chauvinism and fiery leadership. After Penghulu Lawai's sudden death, it was some time before a successor emerged, in the person of Oyang Ajang. By then the Penghulu-ship had gone elsewhere, and it was never recovered. Deprived of the title and regional authority held by Lawai, Oyang Ajang returned to an isolationist rhetoric: let others do as they please, he said, Long Teru would go its own way, as it had always done. Whether Lawai would have taken the same stance we do not know. Certainly he had been a progressive in political terms, but it does not follow that he would have backed religious innovation, especially as Long Teru already had ambivalent relations with the Church.

As far back as the 1930s, Long Teru people had borrowed money from the lone priest resident at the administrative center at Marudi, downriver on the Baram. The priest had, in a modest way, promoted development projects in a couple of the longhouses nearest Marudi. Long Teru people used his support to start rubber plantations, from which, for a while, they did sufficiently well to be able to hire Chinese immigrants to cut the trees for them. At that time, there were even labor lines built behind the longhouse to accommodate the workers. This influx of wealth did not, however, prevent arguments with the priest about repayments of the loan, and after that people at Long Teru showed an indifference to missionaries. This must have caused the poor priest, operating always on a shoestring, to reflect wistfully on the fate of good intentions, but the moment was coming when he would make spectacular conversions among people he had never tried to assist materially. At Long Teru, the incident contributed to an odd blend of political and economic progessivism with tenacious religious conservatism. What held the two together was the Lelak ancestors, and it is no surprise that Kasi was a firm supporter of Oyang Ajang's policies until his death in 1972.

Kasi's vanishing

During the 1970s, however, Kasi began to doubt the viability of the old religion. Already there were a couple of Christian families, and they constituted a fifth column because missionaries would only marry their children if the spouse also converted. Even a tiny minority could disrupt longhouse festivals that were supposed to involve the entire community. Worse, the generation who led the rites were growing older, and the young people were not taking on their responsibilities. Those who had gone away for secondary schooling sometimes seemed uncomfortable with the old ways. Only rarely did Kasi display any bitterness towards young people; she tolerated their affectation of blue jeans and pop music, and laughed with everyone else when, at longhouse parties, they tried to imitate Western dancing – although never with a partner. She concluded, however, that many of them had already effectively severed their links to the ancestors, and that there would be no way back for them.

The final blow was the death of the only shaman she trusted, Tama Ukat Sageng. In contrast to Kasi, his temperament was retiring; even his seances were restrained. Most Berawan shamans (*dayung*) were, in Mircea Eliade's (1964) terms, psychopomps, that is, they became inspired by spirits who danced and sang in their bodies while their own souls journeyed to far realms. Sageng merely sat, chatting with spirit companions unseen by his human audience. Every once in a while, he would turn from speaking to the spirits in their language and ask a question in Berawan, or report a piece of intelligence he had gained from his "Seven Brothers." The effect was both homely and uncanny, and it attached to him outside healing sessions, because he was liable at any time to be in communion with spirits. People at Long Teru regarded him with solicitous pride, a sort of national resource since his reputation extended across the lower Baram region. For many months, I was carefully kept away from his seances in case I did something unexpected and possibly damaging. In the close environment of the longhouse that became increasingly difficult, especially as he was very active, but even after I was admitted Sageng seldom spoke to me. He once made everybody laugh by announcing that I looked like one of the Seven Brothers, and on another occasion he gave me a cheap bead necklace for protection, but mostly he just shot me twinkling smiles – the very embodiment of spiritual power. As I accepted Long Teru's assessment of Kasi's authority, so I shared its sense of awe at Sageng, and the two of them together, next door neighbors and frequent companions, made a powerful coalition. After the coalition was broken, Kasi doubted that any of his several imitators could defend the community. Now, she said, when children are ill, parents will turn to the catechist.

When there was still only a small Christian minority, Kasi resigned herself to the passing of the old ways. She saw a radical break. She did not know, she told me, whether Christians went to the same land of the dead, but she knew where she was going. Much as she loved her children and her grandchildren, her place was with the old ones, her parents and grandparents, and all the Lelak generations who came before.

Kasi also wanted a clean break. She determined that the dignity of the old religion would not be compromised in its passing, and what she had in mind were half-hearted, sloppy, or careless performances of the rituals. Sobriety and solemnity were not the issue; on the contrary, grand rituals had always been synonymous with drinking and noisy conviviality, and they were considered a flop if they did not generate a boisterous vitality bordering on chaos. What bothered her were young people who looked sheepish in front of their schoolfriends, and adults who became timid because they did not know their parts. Their lifeless participation only mocked the drama of the rites that had framed Kasi's life, and the power of the ancestors to whom she felt so close.

Cultural obituaries

Kasi's obstruction of my research was part and parcel of a very literal discourse of the vanishing. To Ivy's account (1995) of Japanese fears of cultural death, the outsider – someone neither Japanese nor cultural critic – is likely to react in disbelief. Surely no country in the world has a more secure cultural identity, manifested in an endless variety of specialized arts, courtly histories, and elaborate etiquettes. By contrast, what I describe is only too believably vanishing. By a coincidence, mortuary rituals stand at the center of Berawan religion, and so I have written extensively about them. Kasi's vision, however, turns my entire research into a kind of drawn-out funeral. Her world was doomed, and I document its demise, a kind of cultural obituary.

My situation is not unique in anthropology; think, for instance, of Raymond Firth's work on Tikopia. Firth picked out the island as a research site precisely because its remoteness promised the opportunity to observe aspects of Polynesian culture no longer found anywhere else, in particular a still-functioning indigenous religion. It is the classic ethnographic motive, and inherently backward-looking, almost as if still caught up with the nineteenth-century evolutionary logic of survivals. Moreover, my use of the term "functioning" is equally provocative because it connotes the standard ethnography of the mid-twentieth century. The fierce revulsion that this style now provokes comes directly from the dead, frozen-under-glass quality that it produces. As has been pointed out a thousand times, to read some of the more wooden studies of African societies produced in the 1950s is to wonder in what marvelous age it all occurred, not a colonial officer or a social problem anywhere in sight! It serves as a warning of the dangers of regnant paradigms.

Consequently, in re-reading *We, the Tikopia* it comes as a surprise to find that early in the book Firth has a long section assessing the impact of missions, trade, new crops, introduced diseases, colonial administration, and overseas labor (1983 [1936]: 31–50). This despite the fact that Tikopia was at the time of Firth's field-work in 1928–9 the archetypal closed community; not much over a thousand people on an island measuring one and a half miles by three, a long ocean voyage from any real land, and visited by ships perhaps once in a year. Nevertheless, half the islanders were already Christian, or at least had been baptized. By the time Firth got around to writing *The Work of the Gods in Tikopia* (1967), it was all a faint memory:

> By the passage of time this book has now acquired the character of an historical document in Polynesian ethnography. The Tikopian religious cycle which, adopting a title from the verna-cular, I termed "Work of the Gods," and which I observed in 1928–9 and again (with James Spillius) in 1952, has now been completely abandoned for more than ten years. That small sector of the Tikopia community which in 1952 still carried out the pagan rites converted to Christianity soon after a disastrous epidemic in 1955. This book then describes a vanished past, a set of institutions not known to many of the young Tikopia themselves.
>
> (1967: v)

Firth himself evokes a musty sense of relics. Against this, however, must be set the amazing fact that his study is absolutely the only ethnographic account that we have of an indigenous Polynesian religion. Such was the early success of missionization that for many Pacific islands we have only the vaguest notion of what went before Christianity, and even in the best cases our reconstruc-tions depend on the reports of travelers, or of converts decades after the fact. By contrast, Firth tell us about rituals of chiefship and the land that still commanded the full allegiances of whole villages, a living religion.

Obviously I defend Firth in order to defend myself; I should be content to accomplish half as much. The issue remains, however, of what could justify ethnographic reportage – Spivak's "information retrieval in silenced areas" (1994: 90) – if it is not to have the air of obituary. Having turned our back on the artificiality of functional stasis, it follows that everything we record is transitory. Even were we to write our ethnographies much more rapidly than we do, we would still be describing what is already gone – old news. Moreover, in a global economy all fieldwork not on Wall Street occurs on some sort of margin, more or less remote. This is the grim specter summoned by many critics of ethnographic methods: nostalgia or irrelevance, or both.

At the same time, however, scholars with very different agendas reach for ethnography as a solution to their own problems. For instance, Chandra Mohanty (1994) critiques what she sees as a monolithic Western feminism, and equates it with a variety of colonial discourse. Its universalizing rhetorics she sees as reductionist: "Men exploit, women are exploited. Such simplistic formulations are both historically reductive; they are also ineffectual in designing strategies to combat oppressions. All they do is reinforce binary divisions between men and women" (1994: 207). What, she asks, would an analysis not caught in such sterile oppositions look like? She answers by way of an example, a study of lace makers in the city of Narsapur, India, made by Maria Mies (1982). At this point the beleaguered anthropologist perks up. Clearly, any activist working with the lace makers could profit from ethnographic information, but it is not clear how Mohanty plans to use it, that is, how she connects the general and the particular. One case would surely be as good as another in undermining "simplistic formulations." There is no question of statistical representativeness. What I hear, in this case and others, is a cautionary tale or parable, an implicit assumption that the world somehow may be shown in a grain of sand, and that also is a familiar anthropological trope; one has only to think of Bronislaw Malinowski's *The Sexual Life of Savages* (1929).

As Clifford (1986) argues, to identify an "ethnographic allegory" is not to equate it with deception. If the logic of preserving what is about to be lost traps anthropologists into certain rhetorics, then the world-in-a-grain-of-sand only provides others, and both have their power.

Indignities

In this case, however, it is not me choosing the allegory, but Kasi. What motivated her, what outraged her, was the progressive trivialization of everything she cared about, and the person who most provoked that reaction was not me and not the teenagers in their blue jeans, but Tama Usang Weng, husband of the frustrated shaman Tina Usang, and spiller of beans about the death songs. Weng was a man not much concerned with dignity. Instead, he exuded enthusiasm, and when he got over-excited, especially if he had been drinking, Kasi's face would harden into a mask of contempt.

Weng believed, in a perfectly straightforward way, that longhouse people could preserve anything they wanted to preserve, if they just took the trouble to teach it to their children. At parties on the veranda, he would appoint himself master of ceremonies, nagging the young people to get up and perform the solo dance called *ngajat*. Etiquette required that no one push themselves forward, and unless there was someone like Weng to incite the crowd no one would come forward. The less accomplished would go first, even very small children being pushed forward for a few minutes, and encouraged vociferously. Finally, the most skilled would be coaxed out, by acclamation, always with much modest confusion. When they began to dance, however, the music was supposed to possess them, and their expressions became contemplative and inward-looking. Both men's and women's styles were elegant and restrained, but the men's was very energetic. Slowly they unwound from a crouching position close to the floor, legs crossed, and rose, swirling, every muscle taut. Then there was a leap and a cry, waving a shield in one hand and a short sword in the other, before spinning again into a tense, poised resting point. For a real exponent, the crowd would sit quietly, occasionally emitting a loud popping sound of delight and admiration, made by pulling the tongue suddenly off the roof of the mouth. After this climax, old people would take a turn, a bit shakier, but still with a few tricks of their own, and no one would hesitate to laugh when they stumbled or yell encouragement when they dared a leap.

In addition to spurring on the dancers, Weng usually supplied the music as well. He was the most accomplished musician at Long Teru, or indeed in any of the Berawan longhouses. For the *ngajat*, he played a three-stringed instrument called *sapé*, sounding a little like a banjo. Its repetitive figures seemed to mesmerize the ablest dancers. Weng was also adept with the *keluné*, a sort of bamboo harmonica, which he played while himself leading a line of dancers, young and old mixed together, everyone copying his steps as he wove along the veranda, changing the step with each new rhythm on his instrument. He could also play a variety of flutes, and a tiny bamboo harp, and sometimes he would pull out an old, very battered accordion that he had been given by an English District Officer many years before. Such was his enthusiasm, Weng even managed to organize parties for no other purpose than to practice dancing. For a Westerner, used to age-segregated social events and teenagers scornful of their elders' tastes, it was surprising to see Weng bustling imperturbably from one longhouse apartment to the next, an angular, quixotic figure, old enough to be their grandfather, cajoling teenagers into putting on their best clothes and joining him on the veranda – surprising, and also I thought admirable (see Figure 12).

Weng saw no reason why the old ways should not persist at Long Teru alone, and he asserted this with no trace of the chauvinism and frustrated ambition that fueled Oyang Ajang's rhetoric. While he restricted himself to *ngajat* and *sapé*, Kasi was supportive, as all the old people were; they loved to see the youngsters vigorous and playful. Even then, Weng would always get carried away, and

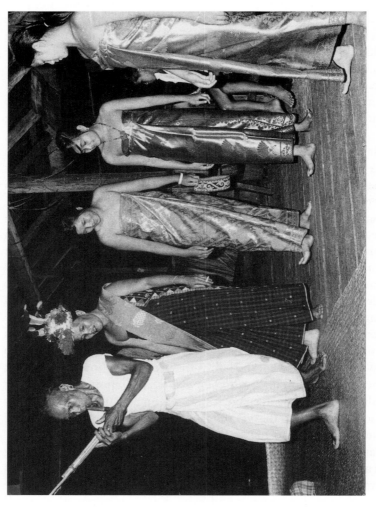

Figure 12 Tama Usang Weng teaching a line dance to young women dressed in their finest sarongs. Photograph by author.

somehow end up by making a fool of himself. Laughter seemed to follow him everywhere, sometimes indulgent, sometimes condescending, and it would not be long before Kasi would begin to frown. The conflict in personal styles invariably came to a head, however, in ritual contexts. At the annual festival, most heads of households offered prayers for the new year in front of their apartments, but Weng always had to erect a prayer station (*tapo'*) of the largest kind (Metcalf 1989: 73–80). He did this out of his usual enthusiasm, but Kasi plainly thought it ostentatious, and indeed presumptuous in a man of no political standing. Hospitality in each room of the longhouse was also a feature of the annual festival, and on one occasion Weng had sampled the rice wine in several before coming to make his prayers. As he waved the sacrificial chicken around, he lost his footing and collapsed into the middle of his prayer station, knocking everything askew. The crowd hooted with laughter, showing no irreligiosity, since prayer sites are not in themselves sacred and no one is required to keep quiet while others pray. Nevertheless, Kasi turned away in disgust.

Weng's boldest project was to revive headhunting rituals that had been defunct for decades. Very abbreviated rites were, in the 1970s, still tagged on to the ends of funerals, but there had once been major festivals of warrior values for which heads were the centerpiece. I triggered this new enthusiasm by asking about the rites, just as I had stimulated Tina Usang's memories of her former glories as a shaman, but others listening in to our conversation also grew excited. Most people at Long Teru knew next to nothing about the rites, while a few remembered seeing them when they were small. Suddenly the popular feeling grew that the rites should be repeated before there was no one left to pass them on. There was, of course, one little problem. The severely abbreviated rites then performed used a bunch of leaves to stand for the new head, but could such a substitute be used for a whole festival? Or could I perhaps borrow a head from somewhere? The idea is not as crazy as it sounds since the Rajah's district officers had on occasions kept a few skulls around that had been confiscated from offending communities, and were subsequently loaned out to cooperating houses in ritual need of them. Nevertheless, there would have been distinctly odd connotations in me producing a skull in the 1970s, even had I been able to acquire one, and this project made me at least as thoughtful as Tina Usang's risky seances had done. The outcome of this enthusiasm is by now predictable. What is surprising is how few people in the longhouse apart from Kasi expressed any misgivings. Clearly they had no idea just how thoroughly headhunting had been sensationalized in the Borneo literature, as demonstrated in the book titles listed in Chapter 1. No one thought of the possibility that stories about renewed head-hunting rites might appear in newspapers on the coast, confirming deeply embedded stereotypes of interior people, and bringing bad publicity to Long Teru. Nor were they suspicious that I might do the same thing, by adding yet another title to the list. There was in the 1970s no tourist industry at all in the Baram watershed, but within the decade it would begin, and the government in Sarawak would be marketing indigenous cultures as relentlessly as the Indonesian government has done for years. There would even be a cultural theme park near the capital, Kuching, with replica longhouses and staged "culture shows," a process that Pemberton (1994: 12) calls "Mini-ization" after the celebrated Taman Mini outside Jakarta. It is not beyond imagining that the revived head-hunting rites might have become a stop on a tourist circuit. Weng would presumably have cheerfully gone on performing them, seeing no problem at all, while his housemates cashed in on the tourist trade, perhaps selling unauthorized copies of my article on the side.

It seems unlikely that Kasi guessed at any of these outcomes. It was sufficient for her that the old ways were subject to purely local indignities. Moreover, no one in the 1970s, myself included, realized how radically the longhouse way of life was about to be changed.

Demolishing "Upriver"

What we did not foresee was the wholesale destruction of the rainforest, made possible by industrial exploitation on a new scale. Commercial logging in itself was not new. For most of the twentieth century, Upriver People had made a small income by extracting the durable *bilian* wood, which furnished house-posts that were virtually immune to rot or termites, and so were in much demand on the coast. But the trees were widely dispersed, and the timber is so heavy that it does not float. Consequently, cutting, sawing, and moving the logs was enormously laborious; it might take weeks to process one tree. Beginning in the 1930s and gathering momentum after the Seond World War, small lumber camps were established downriver in the Baram watershed, moving logs to the coast by drifting them downriver in rafts. An early example near Batu Belah was run by an Englishman, but it was not a success. Later, the investment came from Chinese logging firms already well established and profitable in the Rejang watershed to the south. In the 1970s, work in these camps provided cash income on an irregular basis to some people at Long Teru, and a few men, with their families, spent months at a time away from the longhouse working full-time in the camps, where conditions were usually squalid and schooling unavailable for the children. What limited the scale of these operations was the vagaries of the river itself. Though the huge rafts were a common sight, it took a long time to maneuver them downriver, with diesel tugs constantly straining to keep them from running ashore on one side or the other of the endlessly winding rivers. Low water caused rafts to get stuck; high water made them impossible to control. Meanwhile, the first serious rapids were impassable for the rafts, and we all naively assumed that they would provide a permanent barrier to large-scale cutting of the rainforest.

In the 1980s, these restraints were swept aside. Everything was now on a huge scale: massive earth-moving equipment rapidly extended a network of dirt roads far into the interior, and along them equally massive trucks hauled whole trunks of the giant rain-forest trees directly to transhipment points near the coast. In the space of a decade, the landscape was turned inside out. The rivers that had always provided the arteries of Upriver life suddenly became irrelevant, mere obstacles for the roads, and they ran red with the laterite washing from roads and clearcut wastes.

The capital investment required for exploitation on this scale was commensurably huge, but the profits were even greater. Vast fortunes were made by the timber tycoons of the coast, and their investors in Japan, Hong Kong, and Singapore. Like cocaine in Colombia, such sudden wealth in a poor country distorted all the institutions of civil society. Crooked politicians soon found ways to profit, and used their profits to buy elections. In a gold-rush atmosphere, the conservationist policies of the Forest Department were ignored in a mad dash to cut the forests as rapidly as possible. The ruling clique handed out timber cutting licenses to their immediate family and political lackeys, who promptly auctioned them, growing unimaginably rich virtually overnight. Having worked out the Borneo forests, Malaysian timber companies moved on to New Guinea and South America. Within a generation, profits that might have propelled a steady development policy in Sarawak for a century had fled to Swiss bank accounts, funding lavish lifestyles in Malaysia, London, and Sydney (Brookfield *et al.* 1995; Hong 1987; Hurst 1990).

Needless to say, the money that flowed into Upriver communities was by comparison the merest trickle, but it was enough to transform them. Longhouse apartments were lined with formica, fitted with glass louvered windows, and filled with cheap furniture. Virtually every one had a television and video player. At the same time, however, many longhouses emptied out, as men of working age followed the timber companies deeper into the dwindling forests, or migrated to squatter slums in the coastal cities, principally Miri. With the decline of the timber boom in the mid-1990s, some came back to hang around disconsolately, aware only of their failure to find work in the outside world. Dependence on the cash economy was complete, and the ethos of Upriver life irrevocably changed. Longhouses that had taken days or weeks to reach by river were now a few hours' ride by Landcruiser from Miri, jolting over the rutted logging roads – assuming that transport could be found. What had seemed like the formidable metropolises of independent peoples, each with its own history, became merely inconveniently remote suburbs, home only to the old and unenterprising.

Constructing "Upriver People"

Paradoxically, but not unfamiliarly, the destruction of the Upriver way of life only intensified the self-awareness of Upriver People. The upheavals of the timber boom caused people to mix in new ways in lumber camps and shanty towns, and become aware of a shared predicament. It would be pleasant to report that this translated into a new political consciousness, but that would be overstating the case. There was resistance to the timber companies, in the form of blockades of logging roads, but it occurred in piecemeal fashion and was easily suppressed (Bevis 1995). Some of this resistance was remarkably tenacious in the face of heavy-handed intimidation, but all news of it was kept out of newspapers in Malaysia and Singapore, and stories seldom leaked into the Western press. The blockades sparked no general movement; instead they marked the last desperate struggles of communities that were overwhelmed one after the other.

Consequently, this new awareness had positive and negative aspects. It was the latter that I first noticed. When I went back for extended research in the mid-1990s I tried to round out my picture of regional longhouse dynamics in the last two centuries by visiting a number of communities I had not known well in the 1970s – a typical piece of salvage anthropology. I had assumed, based on past experience, that migration stories were the easiest material to collect, even operating in the Malay lingua franca, but I miscalculated. Suddenly migration stories everywhere had been frustratingly flattened into simple one-step moves out of a homeland in the far interior. Such narrative impoverishment clearly indicated a loss for each community, and I saw nothing else but loss, until a village headman pointed out to me that the old stories were always full of warfare – the strife surrounding the *völkerwanderung* of the nineteenth century – and that people nowadays were uncomfortable talking about that. He himself discouraged the old people from filling the heads of the children with such un-Christian things. History was not being simply forgotten, it was being actively suppressed, or perhaps it might be better to say reworked.

It was during the 1980s that the expression "Upriver People" (*Orang Ulu*) became general; it stopped being simply descriptive, and became unambiguously an ethnic identification. One could not speak of the "invention" of a term like Orang Ulu because it, or something like it, occurs all over Borneo, and indeed much of southeast Asia. Populations are tagged as "upriver" (or inland or mountain) relative to others, but the label has a shifting reference since many people have others both upriver and downriver from themselves. In the present case, however, I can point to one man who was instrumental in making "Orang Ulu" a proper noun. In many ways, he resembled Bilo Kasi's first husband, Penghulu Lawai, in that he showed a mixture of conservative and progressive attitudes, but he had a much longer career, lasting well into the post-independence era, and he was influential over a much wider area, ending up with the title Temenggong, or Paramount Chief. While he was still a Penghulu in the 1950s, Oyong Lawai Jau led many of the Kenyah houses in the upper Baram into Catholicism, and established the main mission station near his own longhouse at Long San. It became a focus of Upriver life, but Oyong Lawai Jau was not content to sit there waiting for visitors. He traveled constantly, even into the Rejang river system to the south, where he had no official authority, and everywhere he used his aristocratic status to promote the notion of a collective Orang Ulu identity. Many educated middle-aged men whom I talked to in the 1990s remembered vividly him appearing at their schools in the towns, rounding up all the longhouse children and haranguing them

Figure 13 Temenggong Oyong Lawai Jau addressing the young men of his longhouse. Photograph by Hedda Morrison, courtesy of Alistair Morrison and the Echols Collection, Division of Rare and Manuscript Collections, Cornell University Library.

about the necessity to apply themselves to their education and never forget their cultural heritage. He even invented a kind of lingua franca of his own, a simplified Kenyah that was apparently comprehensible to most of the children (see Figure 13).

When the term "Orang Ulu" was first promoted in this way, it principally implied the shared cultural background and interwoven histories of the numerous Kayan and Kenyah peoples, and here I must introduce ethnic labels without further ado. After my thorough deconstruction of the terms "Lelak" and "Berawan" in the previous chapter, the reader will no doubt believe me when I say that so loose and encompassing a term as "Kenyah" would take an entire treatise to explain properly. "Kayan" is better, although not without its own complications, but rather than lay them out I shall defer to the existing ethnographic literature, brilliantly summarized in Jérôme Rousseau's *Central Borneo* (1990). What Oyong Lawai Jau saw was the necessity of Kayan and Kenyah people working together if they were ever to have any voice in shaping development policies in the Baram. Almost immediately, however, he and the Orang Ulu National Association that he founded had to deal with ethnic boundaries, and they did no better at it than the anthropologists had done. First there were many groups like the Berawan who were not "really" Kenyah at all, but who were accustomed to being classified that way. That is, Berawan knew perfectly well about the linguistic and cultural gulf that divided them from the followers of Oyong Lawai Jau in the upper Baram (notably, of course, the practice of secondary burial), but they also had to deal with colonial officers who could not get further than a simple dyadic classification of the longhouse peoples. Consequently, the Berawan shrugged and accepted the Kenyah label as being the more elastic of the two.

Incorporating the Berawan and others like them in the Orang Ulu category was consequently easy. The next problem concerned the foraging peoples most often called Penan. For a long time, they did not seem to fit, because they were not thought of as longhouse people. They had in fact been looked down on by longhouse dwellers, but of all the peoples in Baram they put up the stiffest resistance to the loggers. This was surprising since they were not credited with the initiative or ability to organize anything, but they were perhaps the only people who genuinely wanted to preserve the forests as opposed to getting their share of the profits from cutting them. In any event, having lost the fight they were forced into government-built longhouses, so making their Orang Ulu status self-fulfilling.

Next came the people who lived on the plateau at the far headwaters of the Baram, usually called Kelabit. These did not seem to fit because they were not riverine people. Moreover, they had a progressive history of their own, having been among the earliest converts to fundamentalist Christianity, and very active in seeking out higher education for their cleverest children, even sending them overseas. Consequently, some of this educated elite resisted identification with other Upriver People. Nevertheless it has become commonplace to include Kelabit within the *Orang Ulu*, and from the Kelabit, it was an easy step to their cousins to the north in the Limbang and Trusan watersheds. Some of these people anyway already called themselves Lun Dayeh, that being simply "Upriver People" rendered in their own language, and they had done so for generations.

By the 1990s, Oyong Lawai Jau's vision of an Orang Ulu nation had in effect expanded to include everybody in northern Sarawak who was not Malay (i.e. Muslim), not Chinese, and not Iban. Defining it in this way makes its miscellaneous quality obvious. Moreover, it depends on the prior existence of the state of Sarawak, since the term is not used, or not used in the same way, on the other side of the international border in Kalimantan (Indonesian Borneo), though Kayan, Kenyah and Kelabit people live there as well as in Sarawak (Malaysian Borneo), and in even greater numbers. Consequently, you cannot arrive at the category of Upriver People by stacking up some collection of sub-ethnicities; that would not be merely fudging a few details, but would be radically misleading. None of this need surprise us, however, because it only repeats what was true of the other categories – Pelutan, Long Kiput, Kenyah, and all the rest – namely that they are historically contingent.

The question then is what salience the label has, and para-doxically its contrivedness has no bearing on this. Nowadays Long Teru people – or people who used to be from Long Teru – are more likely to identify themselves as Upriver People than as Lelak, Bitokala, Melawan, Berawan, Berawan-Lelak, Kenyah, or any of their other autonyms. This applies in many contexts, particularly in Miri and when talking to non-Orang Ulu, but also amongst themselves in lumber camps and schools. The same is equally true of other Baram peoples, although the term may not have quite the same currency in the adjacent Limbang, Trusan, and Rejang watersheds. Despite its novelty, it is not like one of the neologisms invented by ethnographers, such as Hose's "Klemantan." Even though it was, to some extent, "invented" by Oyong Lawai Jau, it would not have achieved the prominence it now has without some shared historical experience, and it is obvious what that was.

My argument here is the reverse of that made by Anna Tsing for people in the far south of Borneo who call themselves, and are called by others, *Orang Bukit*, i.e. Hill People, rather than Upriver People. She rejects the term because she finds in it the pejorative connotations of "hillbilly." Her reaction had echoes in northern Sarawak. Some of the educated Kelabit elite, conscious of their vanguard position, were uncomfortable describing themselves as "Upriver" people at all, and they thought it foolish that they should name themselves using a phrase borrowed from Malay. These scruples did not, however, occur to most Orang Ulu, and they evidently do not to most Orang Bukit. Nevertheless, Tsing substitutes a term of her own invention, "Meratus Dayaks," naming the inhabitants after the Meratus mountains in which they live (Tsing 1993: 52–3). From my point of view, this is an imposed category with all the disadvantages of "Klemantan." It is a move of a similar kind to the bureaucratic invention of the quasi-geographical term "Appalachia," which Allen Bateau argues (1990) did more harm than good for the poor people in the hills. Moreover, Tsing is forced to include the word "Dayak" in her formula to exclude other kinds of people who happen to live in the mountains, such as Chinese traders. But "Dayak" is classically the term used to lump together all the pagan peoples of interior Borneo, and since colonial times it has had strong connotations of primitiveness. Finally, by imposing this cover term, Tsing erases all the subtle, complicated, fluid, ethnic distinctions discussed in Chapter 4. One of Tsing's reasons for seeing the name "Meratus" as appropriate is that it is a verbal inflection of the word *ratus* (a hundred, or hundreds). These are the "Hundred-ing Mountains" because of the innumerable small ethnic groups found within them, perhaps because the area has been a refuge for indigenous peoples displaced from the lowlands. Tsing gives us no idea, however, how this "hundred-ing" occurred, or what it now signifies in the lives of local people.

It is crucial to note that at least two different processes of "cultural objectification" are at work here. I described in Chapter 4 how longhouse communities were manifested and negotiated through ritual; this was no abstract concept but a specific discourse about what rites, when, and for whom. The same cannot be said for the category Orang Ulu. Although it is important that conversion to Christianity preceded the communal crises of the timber boom, it is clearly not true that whatever new ethnic cohesions emerged were created through religion. For one thing, Upriver People are divided between Catholics and Protestants. Moreover, all the Christian sects to which they belong also have followers from other ethnicities, notably Chinese and Iban.

It follows that other mechanisms were at work, and they resemble those that Richard Handler (1988) describes as formative of Québecois nationalism, in particular the self-conscious attempt by an urban elite to maintain a national heritage seen as threatened, through the organization of cultural events. The Orang Ulu elite came into existence in the 1970s and 1980s. They were to be found mainly in the same coastal city, Miri, that was the new home to longhouse people displaced by the upheavals of the timber boom and living in squatter settlements dotted around the town. The elite were those who had profited from education, just as Oyong Lawai Jau had urged, to obtain white-collar jobs in the civil service, the offshore oil companies, and the professions. Many of them, further heeding the Temenggong's words, felt an urgent need to maintain their contacts with home communities and the emigrants from those communities, and to grasp at something they might call a shared cultural heritage. What surprised me in the 1990s was that marked class differences had not, or had not yet, destroyed the old communal solidarities.

Though they lived in neat cinder-block houses and drove small Japanese cars, the Orang Ulu bourgeoisie maintained their links with their compatriots in the squatter settlements, and saw it as their role to take the lead in organizing gatherings such as Christmas parties that mimicked the communal life of the longhouse veranda. The locales were often church halls, which were also used for classes to teach the youngsters, who knew only city life, such traditional skills as dancing the *ngajat*. Generally speaking, the girls were eager for such instruction, being keen to cultivate the elegant self-presentation and posture of a real Upriver Lady. The boys, however, found the whole process more problematic. Wearing the traditional male loincloth involved displaying more of their buttocks than was consistent with coastal sensibilities, and that made it difficult to coax them into dancing. They made excuses, and slipped away at the first opportunity.

The Sarawak government also looked to the urban elite to organize cultural events. When it was decreed that Upriver People would put on a "culture show" as part of the celebration of the state holiday, they were the ones assigned the job of organizing it. Telephone calls flew back and forth while props and personnel were rounded up and ferried into town, where a stage had been set up. When it came time for the dancing, the girls, though giggling nervously to begin with, carried off the affair with élan. So did some of the older men who had grown up in the longhouse rather than at boarding schools. The town-bred boys suffered badly, however, jiggling about uncomfortably in the middle of the huge stage, conspicuously wearing shorts under their loincloths. It was at about that time that I had learned from someone visiting from Long Teru about Bilo Kasi's illness, and all I could think of, as I suffered for the boys' embarrassment, was how scornfully she would have laughed.

No closure

What this narrative demonstrates is the impossibility of closure. Now that we have rejected closed functionalist systems there can be no completion of circles, and every story leads on to others. Nor, unfortunately, can we abandon realism so far as to conclude that everyone will live happily ever after. It may seem that in the present case at least I can obtain closure in the most time-honored way of all, *Hamlet*-like, by killing off all my heroes and heroines. Weng is long since gone. The death songs of Long Teru are almost as remote a memory as the Work of the Gods in Tikopia, and since I began this essay with Kasi on her deathbed, it ought to be easy enough to write finis. I learned of Kasi's death in 1997 from a letter that described how, according to her instructions, a copy of the book in which I recount the death songs was placed on her chest before the coffin was sealed.

Even here, however, there is a loose end. I still do not know what to make of Kasi's last gesture towards me and, as we know, interpretation never ceases. My first reaction was to be both touched and honored; it seemed to seal a closeness between us. It was not long, however, before I saw other connotations. Perhaps her gesture was a wry comment on what I *failed* to learn, Kasi's last laugh. Although she could not read what was in the book, she knew very well that I never succeeded in transcribing the tapes that I made of the death songs, and since she outlived everyone who might conceivably have helped me do it, she knows I never will. The tapes still exist, but they are useless. Just as Kasi intended, only the ancestors now know exactly what the songs contain. Perhaps it is the tapes that should be with her in the coffin.

Nevertheless, it is the book that is there, so what are the implications of books being used as grave goods? The only things usually put inside coffins – as opposed to hung on mausoleums – are small, crudely carved statuettes that are supposed to represent slaves sent to serve the deceased in the land of the dead. They echo former practices of headhunting and human sacrifice, which were said to have the same effect. Consequently, if the book stands for me, then Kasi evidently has my role in the afterlife assigned. Gripped in a deathly embrace, I am to be carried off into servitude – a sort of cosmic revenge for my arrogance and deviousness. Kasi knew well enough with whom she was going to share the afterlife; perhaps my purgatory will be to repeat to those robust spirits the contents of the death songs, as I did that night for Kasi, while they guffaw hugely.

Despite the novelty of books as grave goods, however, there are certain connotations that make them appropriate, connotations of processing, refinement, and condensation. My account of Berawan death rites is that they constitute a kind of ancestor factory. Over months or years, the corpse is ritually processed, stage by stage, from the putrescent corpse until the dry and disarticulated bones can finally be stored in a valuable jar in a fine mausoleum. The book took even longer to produce; is it possible that Kasi had any idea of me poring over fieldnotes and slowly writing a manuscript, or of the glacial pace of publication? That may stretch credulity, but Kasi's generation certainly attributed considerable power to the written word, as a direct result of the archival administrative style of English colonialism described by Bernard Cohn (1996: 16–56) – and all the more so if they were illiterate themselves. Consequently, the book may have had for Kasi the kind of condensed power she associated with ancestral relics. Perhaps Kasi has set a precedent, and the speakers of the prayers collected in another book will soon be clamoring for copies.

Can it be that Kasi is glad, after all, that the book exists? She may at last relax her vigilance in preserving the dignity of the old rites; there is now no risk that they will be performed in some half-hearted way, nor that one of Tama Usang Weng's gaffes will provoke laughter. Moreover, there is in the book a photograph of Kasi in her youth, and I like to think that it appeals to her vanity. Perhaps she is pleased at the prospect of showing the book off to her parents and grandparents. Or do I still hear the echo of that disapproving voice that so abruptly terminated Tina Usang's shamanistic revival? If the book is a distillate of many acts of narration, if it seems to stake a definite claim to represent the rites, why should not Kasi take back what was always already hers? Between these poles, smiling or frowning, affectionate or severe, your judgment is now as good as mine. Beyond that there is no knowing, and, having paused to wonder, we shall have to get on. *Malut dé, malut kita.*

Notes

1 Lies

1 *The Jungle Book* was not well known in North America until the recent appearance of the Disney version, but it has been a popular children's book in Britain for over a century. What does not come across in the animated version is the colonial context of the story. The child Mowgli's relationship with the animals as arbiter and guide is an animistic version of the idealized relationship of the British to the subject peoples of the Raj.

2 Needless to say, I was the frequent butt of these sessions. My ineptness at walking down slippery logs leading to the river's edge was legendary, and having everyone imitate my wobbly moves could keep a longhouse party laughing for half an hour. So used was I to this that I cannot imagine fieldwork in a place where people act with reserve towards the ethnographer.

3 This is not to suggest that there is no didactic function in fairy stories as we know them in the West. Even the most admonitory, however, such as Pinocchio and his lengthening nose, have a very different tone to Kasi's narrating.

4 The item nicely demonstrates the modus operandi of the tabloid press. To make one headline story involves mixing a cocktail of sensational features: Martians, Borneo headhunting, and South American head shrinking. The illustration showed one of the little black plastic heads with long black hair often sold alongside Halloween props.

2 Struggle

1 I should note that this total includes two small grants, one of which did come from the NSF. It was, however, only to cover photographic and recording equipment. The other subsidiary grant came from the Wenner-Gren Foundation, one of the very few private foundations specializing in the support of anthropological research.

2 The narrative of this struggle has already appeared in an article (1998). I have chosen to do without the usual pages of acknowledgements at the beginning of the book because they are nowadays mostly a way of name-dropping; they serve to show how many important people the author knows. My only regret is that I consequently failed to acknowledge the help of Dan Segal, then editor of *Cultural Anthropology*. Had he not shown an interest in the shorter version of the story, I would not have proceeded with this essay.

3 Power

1 There was only one occasion when I was briefly the focus of real animosity in the longhouse. To get through longhouse parties that lasted days, I used sometimes to take a sleeping pill, allowing me to doze off for at least a couple of hours. A young man wishing to copy my technique got hold of the pills, and for good measure took several. He dropped into a deep sleep, and there was a tense time until I could get him to sit up and talk.

2 Rodney Needham points out to me that Geertz is wrong in one important particular about Evans-Pritchard's account of the campaign against the Italians in Ethiopia. Geertz assumes that his stories were "polished from many bar-room tellings," but like many of his generation in Britain, Evans-Pritchard never talked about his wartime experiences.

3 That postcolonial studies has now become a mature field is indicated by the large number of readers on the topic that have appeared recently, including: Ashcroft *et al.* (1995), Cooper and Stoler (1997), McClintock *et al.* (1997), Mongia (1996), Prakash (1995), Williams and Chrisman (1994).

4 The predicament of the veranda ethnographer in terms of languages is not unlike the English District Officer presiding at his court.

Though he had all power of decision, he could often not follow the testimony, and so was at the mercy of court interpreters who might very well have their own agendas.

5 I cannot say that anyone in the picture was forced to drink in this way, but I have certainly seen it done, for instance with missionaries who claimed to be teetotalers.

6 The District Officer in question was Donald Hudden, who was still in Baram when the Japanese arrived in 1942. He fled upriver, and was hidden for a while near Long Teru. But Hudden feared that people at Long Teru would be punished, so he moved further inland. Some months later he was followed and murdered by a group of Iban, who took his head to the Japanese for a reward.

7 This studio was located in Marudi, and run by a local Chinese photographer who was active in the 1950s and 1960s. I have seen many of his pictures in longhouses, often posed against a canvas backdrop showing a classical landscape with a Roman temple. Unfortunately, my efforts to find the man himself and his collection did not succeed. He was unmarried, and something of a loner, and I have no idea what happened to his negatives.

4 Ethnicity

1 Even though Long Teru is now a backwater, and not at all a center of transportation, it is still shown, for instance, in the *Times Atlas of the World*, one of only half a dozen places named in the whole Baram watershed.

2 Genealogies reveal that many couples at this time had no children, and I can offer no explanation for this. The same pattern affected many of the smaller ethnic groups in the lower Baram, making what were already marginal people much more vulnerable to assimilation. My only clue is that there were abortifacients used to prevent illegitimate births, and these may have had permanently damaging effects.

3 The most elite families were always the ones most inclined to marry out of their own community. In his report on research possibilities in Sarawak, Edmund Leach (1950: 52) reports a case of two full brothers and a first cousin, each married into different longhouses and leaders of three supposedly different ethnic groups. In recent

decades, the tendency to marry out has become world-wide in its scope. It is noticeable that many of the children of the most prestigious aristocrats married Westerners (British, Americans, and French) often as a result of relationships begun during education overseas.

5 Closure

1 Unlike the Pelutan, whose name I have not seen in print, there are a few references to the Lelak. They are insufficient, however, to furnish any useful picture.
2 The same is not true elsewhere. As Jérôme Rousseau (1998) shows, the Kayan of the Belaga (upper Rejang) have tenaciously hung on to their version of Bungan, which they describe as the ideal religion.

References

Asad, Talal (1973) "Introduction," in Talal Asad (ed.) *Anthropology and the Colonial Encounter* (pp. 9–20). Atlantic Highlands, NJ: Humanities.

Ashcroft, Bill, Griffiths, Gareth, and Tiffin, Helen (1995) *The Post-Colonial Studies Reader*. London: Routledge.

Bakhtin, Mikhail (1986) *Speech Genres and Other Late Essays*. Austin: University of Texas Press.

Barrett, David (1993) *Uncertain Warriors: Lyndon Johnson and his Vietnam Advisors*. Lawrence: University Press of Kansas Press.

Barth, Frederik (1969) *Ethnic Groups and Boundaries*. Boston: Little Brown.

Bateau, Allen (1990) *The Invention of Appalachia*. Tucson: University of Arizona Press.

Bateson, Gregory (1958) *Naven*. Second edition. Stanford, CA: Stanford University Press.

Berreman, Gerald (1969) "Not So Innocent Abroad," *Nation*, November 10: 505–9.

Bevis, William (1995) *Borneo Log: The Struggle for Sarawak's Forests*. Seattle: University of Washington Press.

Brightman, Robert (1995) "Forget Culture: Replacement, Transcendence, Relexification," *Cultural Anthropology* 10: 509–46.

Brookfield, Harold, Potter, Lesley, and Byron, Yvonne (1995) *In Place of the Forest: Environmental and Socio-economic Transformation in Borneo and the Eastern Malay Peninsula*. Tokyo: United Nations University Press.

Brown, Donald (1970) *Brunei: The Structure and History of a Bornean Malay Sultanate.* Brunei: Monographs of the Brunei Museum no. 2.

Brown, Richard (1973) "Anthropology and Colonial Rule: Godfrey Wilson and the Rhodes–Livingstone Institute, Northern Rhodesia," in Talal Asad (ed.) *Anthropology and the Colonial Encounter* (pp. 173–98). Atlantic Highlands, NJ: Humanities.

Brumann, Christoph (1999) "Writing for Culture: Why a Successful Concept Should Not be Discarded," *Current Anthropology* 40: S1–S27.

Burrows, J.W. (1966) *Evolution and Society: A Study of Victorian Social Theory.* Cambridge: Cambridge University Press.

Cable, Larry (1986) *Conflict of Myths: The Development of American Counterinsurgency Doctrine and the Vietnam War.* New York: University of New York Press.

Carsten, Janet and Hugh-Jones, Stephen (eds) (1995) *About the House: Lévi-Strauss and Beyond.* Cambridge: Cambridge University Press.

Casagrande, Joseph (ed.) (1960) *In the Company of Man: Twenty Portraits by Anthropologists.* New York: Harper.

Clifford, James (1986) "On Ethnographic Analogy," in James Clifford and George Marcus (eds) *Writing Culture: The Poetics and Politics of Ethnography* (pp. 98–121). Berkeley: University of California Press.

Cohn, Bernard (1996) *Colonialism and its Forms of Knowledge: The British in India.* Princeton, NJ: Princeton University Press.

Cooper, Frederick and Stoler, Ann (eds) (1997) *Tensions of Empire: Colonial Cultures in a Bourgeois World.* Berkeley: University of California Press.

Danziger, Eve (1997) "To Play a Speaking Part: Fantasy, Falsehood, and Fiction in Mopan Maya." Seminar paper delivered at the University of Virginia. (A revised version in press with *American Anthropologist.*)

Department of the Army (1962) *Counterguerrilla Operations.* Field Manual 31-16. Washington, DC: Department of the Army.

DePaulo, Bella, Kashy, Deborah, Kirkendol, Susan, Wyer, Melissa, and Epstein, Jennifer (1996) "Lying in Everyday Life," *Journal of Personality and Social Psychology* 70: 979–95.

Déscola, Philippe (1992) "Societies of Nature and the Nature of Society," in Adam Kuper (ed.) *Conceptualizing Society* (pp. 107–22). London: Routledge.

Domalain, Jean-Yves (1974) *Panjamon: I Was a Headhunter*. New York: Warner.

Dumont, Jean-Paul (1978) *The Headman and I: Ambiguity and Ambivalence in the Fieldwork Experience*. Chicago: Waveland.

Eliade, Mircea (1964) *Shamanism: Archaic Techniques of Ecstasy*. New York: Pantheon.

Engelke, Matthew (1998) Transcript of interviews with Edith Turner. Unpublished MS.

Eriksen, Thomas (1993) *Ethnicity and Nationalism*. London: Pluto.

Firth, Raymond (1983) [1936] *We, The Tikopia: A Sociological Study of Kinship in Primitive Polynesia*. Stanford: Stanford University Press.

—— (1967) *The Work of the Gods in Tikopia*. London: Athlone Press.

Fortes, Meyer (1940) "The Political System of the Tallensi of the Northern Territories of the Gold Coast," in Meyer Fortes and Edward Evans-Pritchard (eds) *African Political Systems* (pp. 239–71). Oxford: Oxford University Press.

Frazer, James (1922) *The Golden Bough*. Abridged edition. New York: Macmillan.

Geddes, William (1957) *Nine Dayak Nights*. Melbourne: Oxford University Press.

Geertz, Clifford (1988) *Works and Lives: The Anthropologist as Author*. Stanford: Stanford University Press.

Georges, E. (1990) *The Making of a Transnational Community: Migration, Development and Cultural Change in the Dominican Republic*. New York: Columbia University Press.

Glick, N., Basch, L., and Blanc-Szanton, C. (eds) (1992) *Towards a Transnational Perspective on Migration: Race, Class, Ethnicity and Nationalism Reconsidered*. New York: New York Academy of Sciences.

Gluckman, Max (1965) *Politics, Law and Ritual in Tribal Society*. Chicago: Aldine.

Goffman, Erving (1963) *Behavior in Public Places*. New York: Free Press.

Gough, Kathleen (1968) "New Proposals for Anthropologists," *Current Anthropology* 9: 403–7.

Hall, Stuart (1996) "Cultural Identity and Diaspora," in Padmini Mongia (ed.) *Contemporary Postcolonial Theory: A Reader* (pp. 108–25). London: Arnold.

Handler, Richard (1988) *Nationalism and the Politics of Culture in Quebec*. Madison: University of Wisconsin Press.

Haraway, Donna (1991) "Situated Knowledges: The Science Question in Feminism and the Privilege of Partial Perspective," in *Simians, Cyborgs, and Women: The Reinvention of Nature* (pp. 183–202). New York: Routledge.

Hays, Terence (ed.) (1992) *Ethnographic Presents: Pioneering Anthropologists in the Papua New Guinea Highlands*. Berkeley: University of California Press.

Headland, Thomas (ed.) (1992) *The Tasaday Controversy: Assessing the Evidence*. Washington, DC: American Anthropology Association.

Hong, Evelyne (1987) *Natives of Sarawak: Survival in Borneo's Vanishing Forests*. Penang: Institut Masyarakat.

Hooper, Anthony and Huntsman, Judith (1973) "A Demographic History of the Tokelau Islands," *Journal of the Polynesian Society* 82: 366–411.

Hose, Charles (1927) *Fifty Years of Romance and Research, or, The Diary of a Jungle Wallah*. London: Hutchinson.

Hose, Charles and McDougall, William (1912) *The Pagan Tribes of Borneo*, Vols I and II. London: Macmillan.

Hsu, Francis (1948) *Under the Ancestors' Shadow: Chinese Culture and Personality*. Stanford, CA: Stanford University Press.

Hurst, Philip (1990) *Rainforest Politics: Ecological Destruction in Southeast Asia*. London: Zed Press.

Hutchinson, John and Smith, Anthony (eds) (1996) *Ethnicity*. Oxford: Oxford University Press.

Hymes, Dell (1968) "Linguistic Problems in Defining the Concept of 'Tribe,'" in June Helm (ed.) *Essays on the Problem of the Tribe* (pp. 46–68). Seattle: University of Washington Press.

Ivy, Marilyn (1995) *Discourses of the Vanishing: Modernity, Phantasm, Japan*. Chicago: University of Chicago Press.

James, Wendy (1973) "The Anthropologist as Reluctant Imperialist," in Talal Asad (ed.) *Anthropology and the Colonial Encounter* (pp. 41–70). Atlantic Highlands, NJ: Humanities.

Jones, E. (1979) "The Rocky Road from Acts to Dispositions," *American Psychologist* 34: 107–17.

Kashy, Deborah and DePaulo, Bella (1996) "Who Lies?," *Journal of Personality and Social Psychology* 70: 1037–51.

Kelly, Amy (1971) *Eleanor of Aquitaine and the Four Kings.* Cambridge: Harvard University Press.

Kennedy, Raymond (1974) *Bibliography of Indonesian Peoples and Cultures.* New Haven, CT: Yale University Press.

Kunhardt, Phillip, Jr, Kunhardt, Phillip, III, and Kunhardt, Peter (1995) *P.T. Barnum: America's Greatest Showman.* New York: Knopf.

Kuper, Adam (1973) *Anthropologists and Anthropology: The British School 1922–1972.* New York: Pica.

Lakoff, George and Johnson, Mark (1980) *Metaphors We Live By.* Chicago: University of Chicago Press.

Langer, Elinor (1967) "Foreign Research: CIA Plus Camelot Equals Trouble for US Scholars," *Science* 156: 1583–4.

Leach, Edmund (1950) *Social Science Research in Sarawak.* London: Colonial Office.

—— (1961) *Rethinking Anthropology.* London: Athlone Press.

Lebar, Frank (ed.) (1972) *Ethnic Groups of Insular Southeast Asia,* Vol. I. New Haven, CT: Human Relations Area File.

Levin, Charles and Kroker, Arthur (1984) "Baudrillard's Challenge," *Canadian Journal of Political and Social Theory* 8: 5–18.

Lévi-Strauss, Claude (1967) *Structural Anthropology.* New York: Doubleday.

—— (1968) *The Savage Mind.* Chicago: University of Chicago Press.

Lloyd, T.O. (1984) *The British Empire 1558–1983.* Oxford: Oxford University Press.

Lyotard, Jacques (1984) *The Postmodern Condition: A Report on Knowledge.* Minneapolis: University of Minnesota Press.

McClintock, Anne, Mufti, Aamir, and Shohat, Ella (eds) (1997) *Dangerous Liaisons: Gender, Nation and Postcolonial Perspectives.* Minneapolis: University of Minnesota Press.

McLean, Ann (1992) "In the Footprints of Reo Fortune," in Terence Hays (ed.) *Ethnographic Presents: Pioneering Anthropologists in the Papua New Guinea Highlands* (pp. 37–67). Berkeley: University of California Press.

McLuhan, Marshall with Fiore, Quentin (1969) *The Medium is the Massage: An Inventory of Effects.* New York: Bantam Book.

Macpherson, C. (1976) "Polynesians in New Zealand: An Emerging Eth-class?," in D. Pitt (ed.) *Social Class in New Zealand* (pp. 99–112). Auckland: Longman Paul.

Malinowski, Bronislaw (1929) *The Sexual Life of Savages*. New York: Harcourt, Brace.

—— (1954) *Magic, Science and Religion and Other Essays*. New York: Doubleday.

Marcus, George (1995) "Ethnography in/of the World System: The Emergence of Multi-sited Ethnography," *Annual Reviews in Anthropology* 24: 95–117.

Marcus, George and Fischer, Michael (1986) *Anthropology as Cultural Critique: An Experimental Moment in the Social Sciences*. Chicago: University of Chicago Press.

Mead, Margaret (1923) *Coming of Age in Samoa*. New York: William Morrow.

Melland, Frank (1923) *In Witch-Bound Africa: An Account of the Primitive Kaonde Tribe and Their Beliefs*. London: Seeley, Service and Co.

Metcalf, Peter (1976) "Who are the Berawan? Ethnic Classification and the Distribution of Secondary Treatment of the Dead in Central Northern Borneo," *Oceania* XLVII: 85–105.

—— (1982) *A Borneo Journey into Death: Berawan Eschatology from Its Rituals*. Philadelphia: University of Pennsylvania Press.

—— (1989) *Where are YOU/SPIRITS: Style and Theme in Berawan Prayer*. Washington, DC: Smithsonian.

—— (1992) "Aban Jau's Boast," *Representations* 37: 136–50.

—— (1996) "Images of Headhunting," in Janet Hoskins (ed.) *Headhunting and the Social Imagination in Southeast Asia* (pp. 249–90). Stanford, CA: Stanford University Press.

—— (1998) "The Book in the Coffin: On the Ambiguities of 'Informants'," *Cultural Anthropology* XIII: 326–43.

Metge, Joan (1964) *A New Maori Migration*. London: Athlone Press.

Mies, Maria (1982) *The Lace Makers of Narsapur: Indian Housewives Produce for the World Economy*. London: Zed Press.

Mohanty, Chandra (1994) "Under Western Eyes: Feminist Scholarship and Colonial Discourse," in Patrick Williams and Laura Chrisman (eds) *Colonial Discourse and Post-Colonial Theory: A Reader* (pp. 196–220). New York: Columbia University Press.

Mongia, Padmini (ed.) (1996) *Contemporary Postcolonial Theory: A Reader*. London: Arnold.

Moore-Gilbert, Bart (1997) *Postcolonial Theory: Contexts, Practices, Politics*. London: Verso.

Needham, Rodney (1973) "The Left Hand of the Mugwe: An Analytical Note on the Structure of Meru Symbolism," in Rodney Needham (ed.) *Right and Left: Essays on Dual Symbolic Classification* (pp. 109–27). Chicago: University of Chicago Press.

O'Brian, Patrick (1970) *Master and Commander*. New York: Norton.

Parry, Richard (1998) "What Young Men Do," *Granta* 62: 83–124.

Passaro, Joanne (1997) "You Can't Take the Subway to the Field! 'Village' Epistemologies in the Global Village," in Akhil Gupta and James Ferguson (eds) *Anthropological Locations: Boundaries and Grounds of a Field Science* (pp. 147–62). Berkeley: University of California Press.

Pemberton, John (1994) *On the Subject of "Java."* Ithaca, NY: Cornell University Press.

Pigafetta, Antonio (1525?) *Primo Viaggio intorno al Mondo*. (First Voyage around the World) in Emma Blai and James Robertson (eds) (1903–9) *The Philippine Islands, 1493–1803: Explorations by Early Navigators, Descriptions of the Islands and their Peoples, their History and Records of the Catholic mission, as related in Contemporaneous Books and Manuscripts, Showing the Political, Economic, Commercial and Religious Conditions of those Islands from the Earliest Relations with European Nations to the Beginning of the Nineteenth Century*, vols XXXIII: 25–267, XXXIV: 38–180. Cleveland: A.H. Clarke.

Prakash, Gyan (ed.) (1995) *After Colonialism: Imperial Histories and Postcolonial Displacements*. Princeton, NJ: Princeton University Press.

Reece, Robert (1982) *The Name of Brooke: The End of White Rajah Rule in Sarawak*. Kuala Lumpur: Oxford University Press.

Rogel-Rara, Amelia and Nabayra, Emmanuel (1992) "The Genealogical Evidence," in Thomas Headland (ed.) *The Tasaday Controversy: Assessing the Evidence* (pp. 89–106). Washington, DC: American Anthropological Association.

Room, Adrian (1999) *Brewer's Dictionary of Phrase and Fable*. Millennium Edition London: Casell.

Rosenau, Pauline (1992) *Post-modernism and the Social Sciences: Insights, Inroads, and Intrusions*. Princeton, NJ: Princeton University Press.

Rousseau, Jérôme (1990) *Central Borneo: Ethnic Identity and Social Life in a Stratified Society*. Oxford: Clarendon Press.

—— (1998) *Kayan Religion: Ritual Life and Religious Reform in Central Borneo*. Leiden: KITLV Press.

Runciman, Steven (1960) *The White Rajahs: A History of Sarawak from 1841 to 1946*. Cambridge: Cambridge University Press.

Said, Edward (1978) *Orientalism*. New York: Vintage.

—— (1994) *Culture and Imperialism*. New York: Vintage.

St John, Spenser (1862) *Life in the Forests of the Far East*, Vols I and II. London: Smith.

Salemink, Oscar (1991) "*Mois* and *Maquis*: The Invention and Appropriation of Vietnam's Montagnards from Sabatier to the CIA," in George Stocking (ed.) *Colonial Situations: Essays on the Contextualization of Ethnographic Knowledge* (pp. 243–83). Madison: University of Wisconsin Press.

Salmond, Anne (1975) *Hui: A Study of Maori Ceremonial Gatherings*. Wellington: Reed.

Schenkler, B. and Leary, M. (1982) "Social Anxiety and Self Presentation," *Psychological Bulletin* 92: 641–69.

Scholes, Robert (1989) *Protocols of Reading*. New Haven, CT: Yale University Press.

Scott, James (1984) *Everyday Forms of Peasant Resistance*. New Haven, CT: Yale University Press.

—— (1986) "Everyday Forms of Peasant Resistance," in James Scott and Benedict Kerkvleit (eds) *Everyday Forms of Peasant Resistance in Southeast Asia* (pp. 5–35). London: Cass.

Scott, James and Kerkvleit, Benedict (eds) (1986) *Everyday Forms of Peasant Resistance in Southeast Asia*. London: Cass.

Smith, W. Robertson (1889) *Lectures on the Religion of the Semites: First Series, The Fundamental Institutions*. Edinburgh: A. and C. Black.

Spivak, Gayatri (1994) "Can the Subaltern Speak?," in Patrick Williams and Laura Chrisman (eds) *Colonial Discourse and Post-Colonial Theory: A Reader* (pp. 66–111). New York: Columbia University Press.

Stocking, George (ed.) (1983) *Observers Observed: Essays on Ethnographic Fieldwork*. Madison: University of Wisconsin Press.

Stoler, Ann (1991) "Carnal Knowledge and Imperial Power: Gender, Race and Morality in Colonial Asia," in Micaela di Leonardo (ed.) *Gender at the Crossroads of Knowledge: Feminist Anthropology in the Postmodern Era* (pp. 51–101). Berkeley: University of California Press.

Sutton, C. and Chaney, E. (eds) (1987) *Caribbean Life in New York City: Sociocultural Dimensions*. New York: Center for Migration Studies.

Tambiah, Stanley J. (1976) *World Conqueror and World Renouncer: A Study of Buddhism and Polity in Thailand against a Historical Background*. Cambridge: Cambridge University Press.

Tsing, Anna (1993) *In the Realm of the Diamond Queen*. Princeton, NJ: Princeton University Press.

Turner, Edith (1987) *The Spirit and the Drum: A Memoir of Africa*. Tucson: University of Arizona Press.

Turner, Victor (1957) *Schism and Continuity in an African Society*. Manchester: Manchester University Press.

—— (1967) *The Forest of Symbols: Aspects of Ndembu Ritual*. Ithaca, NY: Cornell University Press.

—— (1974) *Dramas, Fields, and Metaphors: Symbolic Action in Human Society*. Ithaca, NY: Cornell University Press.

Tylor, Edward Burnett (1964) [1878] *Researches into the Early History of Mankind and the Development of Civilization*. Abridged version. Chicago: University of Chicago Press.

Vattimo, Gianni (1988) *The End of Modernity: Nihilism and Hermeneutics in Post-Modern Culture*. Cambridge: Polity.

Wagner, Roy (1975) *The Invention of Culture*. Chicago: University of Chicago Press.

Wilde, Oscar (1994) [1891] "The Decay of Lying," in Richard Ellman (ed.) *The Artist as Critic: Critical Writings of Oscar Wilde* (pp. 290–320). New York: Random House.

Williams, Patrick and Chrisman, Laura (eds) (1994) *Colonial Discourse and Post-Colonial Theory: A Reader*. New York: Columbia University Press.

Young, Michael (ed.) (1979) *The Ethnography of Malinowski*. London: Routledge.

Index